Fearful Dog Rehabilitation

Life with a Puppy Farm Rescue

by

Sally Gutteridge

Copyright

Interior Layout: Sandeep Likhar

Books may be purchased by contacting the publisher and author at:
info@sallygutteridge.com
www.sallygutteridge.com

Imprint: Independently published
© 2018 by Sally Gutteridge.
All rights reserved.

For Lacy, Penny and Holly, three little ladies that showed me how easy it is to sparkle when you're loved!

Table of Contents

Introduction

Everyone loves puppies! A new life, a bundle of fluff and that clean smell. How could we not be drawn to the puppy across the room, street or park? There are people that know this though and they monetise that tiny life ten or a hundredfold, with large breeding areas where parent dogs produce puppies time and again.

It's the parent dogs that we are covering in this book; to be exact the escapees who get a second chance at life as it always should have been for them. We are going to explore who they are, how to help them, and the environment they will need in order to rebalance and heal.

Fixing a dog who has struggled for all of their life is possible. In fact, it's easy when we know how because, in the right environment, they fix themselves. All we need to do is learn how to provide that environment, properly communicate with them, and be worthy of their trust in a way that they can understand.

Chapter One: Origins

"Dogs have a way of finding the people who need them, and filling an emptiness we didn't ever know we had."
— Thom Jones

It's a dark winter evening and our little two human and four dog family are (somewhat embarrassingly) watching Most Haunted. The program is set in an abandoned prison, only the humans in the house are awake. As the "excitement" in the program rises, with much squealing from a terrified Yvette - with little evidence why - large metal doors start banging. That's when the real horror begins.

Holly, our tiny Yorkshire Terrier jumps awake and starts running in different directions in the room, her panic obvious. Off went the TV as we got another taste of the first few years of her life, Holly had grown up in a puppy farm. She's been with us for over two years now and is our third ex-breeding dog. A tiny Yorkie fetched out at six years old with a double hernia and total muscle wastage, she's become a little plump lump full of life and merriment. Holly is a success story and an escapee that you will get to know more of throughout the book. First though, let's take a look at where she came from.

There are hundreds, perhaps thousands of farmed dogs in the UK alone, many more scattered across the world. Puppies are big business because of the unique relationship that dogs and people share.

About Farming

Breeding animals for their bodies, babies, or even bodily fluids has been given the name farming. Yet the reality is a little different. Farming has to be sustainable or people wouldn't do it. It needs a good profit margin, which means the difference between the cash the farmer puts in and the cash they get out. Farming of animals for meat and milk is dwindling in 2019 as people choose plant foods for health and ethics. Veganism, (removal of all animal products from the diet including dairy and eggs) has grown fourfold in the past four years from 150,000 to 600,000, according to the Vegan Society. The UK Government subsidises farming and in many cases the subsidisation currently makes up more of a farmer's income than the role itself.

With the profit of farming falling, and the ever-increasing strength of a human and dog relationship, some farmers have added to their income by breeding dogs for sale. Other puppy farmers have never used other animals yet create big breeding establishments with hundreds of dogs.

Dog breeders are varied. Some do it in their homes and raise one or two litters in a mother dog's lifetime, ensuring that puppies are healthy, socialised, and genetically well. This prepares the puppy for life as a family dog as well as it possibly can. This dog breeder acknowledges their ethical responsibility to every puppy they facilitate into life. They interview potential homes with high detail and with conviction. This type of breeder will usually have lifetime homes ready before the puppies are even born. They also insist that their puppies are not bred from and ensure contracts are signed that if the dog can no longer be kept, they will be returned to the place their lives began.

 The interim breeder is one that has litters in their backyard or part of their home. For cash, this type of breeder may not interact with the dogs and will often not meet their needs. Often seeing the dog as a commodity, yet without being outwardly cruel to them. We rescued a little Yorkie from this type of situation once, Penny (left) was abandoned

with four sisters in an empty house, when her breeding days were over. She had no fear of people and after joining us lived a happy life, despite a significant heart murmur until her time to leave us came.

The other breeder type is the puppy farmer, who is as far away from being ethically-driven as it's possible to be.

The Puppy Farm

A puppy farm is usually licenced by the local council in its geographical area as a legal breeding establishment. Licencing officers visit and grant a licence to this type of breeder making the whole thing legal. There are a number of rules that licencing is supposed to be based on canine welfare, but the guidelines vary and don't reach the dizzy heights of even the most basic life quality for the dogs.

I have never been inside a puppy farm but have carried out some research from others who have. Remember as you read the following descriptions that someone has licenced most puppy farms as acceptable practice; they are currently legal.

The commercial puppy farm is big, there can be hundreds of dogs in one. There is a lot of noise and distress from the dogs. Doors bang and cages rattle, there are sounds of tiny puppies at all different ages – simply being puppies. The smell of urine can be recognised from outside and is overwhelming inside. The dogs are covered in urine, matted, unhealthy, and desperately sad. Puppy farm parents have bodies that are ravaged by breeding; they have many litters that are forcibly removed and then mated again. When they reach the end of their breeding life some go to rescue whilst others are killed. One person who shared her experience with me said that the dogs were clubbed to death when they were no longer of use. Dogs are our friends. They have evolved as companions, workmates, and partners for people, yet some of our own species do this to them, whilst our own government provides legal back-up via licencing. All based on cash.

In the last couple of years, though, the plight of the farmed dog has been publicised, and slowly, changes are being made. We are starting to see animal welfare awareness, questions asked about dogs sold in pet stores, and even the cessation of third parts sales of puppies. In Scotland it's illegal to sell puppies in pet stores and the same legal stance is currently being set in England, too.

I don't believe that you or I could even imagine how it must feel to be in that situation, as a puppy farm parent dog. Which is why the resilience of the escapees is heartening. The domestic dog wants a person. No matter what we have done to them in their past, dogs will choose a person and become theirs. Then when that person shows kindness and earns their trust, this dog will sparkle.

The Puppies

Puppy farmers know that people would run for miles and tell anyone listening if they were shown into the breeding environment to choose their new family member, so they get sneaky about selling the little lives that they facilitate.

One of the people I spoke to said they went to a house of a highly recommended breeder and chose their puppy in a clean, warm house. When they went back to collect their puppy they couldn't find the breeder so explored, then they found the farm, tucked around the back of the house. They then realised that the smell of urine was not the working farm nearby, but the puppy farm itself. The noise was deafening, the smell putrid, and the air filled with sounds of desperation.

Puppy farmers use host families with excuses as to why the parents are not around. They offer to deliver puppies to your home, meet in hotels, and even at train stations. The thing that makes this process easy for them is that once a puppy of six to eight weeks old has been given a bath, they will usually look healthy and not give much away about their sinister beginnings.

Whilst a farmed puppy may look perfect at the time we meet him, there's a lot more going on inside the dog that undoubtedly will appear, through his health and behaviour. This is because a puppy at six to eight weeks old is not a blank canvas. In fact, even a puppy at a few hours old is not even a blank canvas. A dog's personality starts to develop at the moment he is conceived and the building blocks for that personality come directly from the life and health of his parents and grandparents. This fact is exactly why people may buy a puppy from a stranger, think they will get a nice family dog and end up with an adolescent dog who is nervy, scared, and probably also physically ill.

Puppies are conceived through a process called meiosis, which is how all animals that reproduce sexually have babies. Meiosis ensures that the puppy inherits half of his DNA from mother and half from father. Both parents have received half their DNA from their own mom and dad in the same way, so puppy gets a quarter of each grandparents' traits.

DNA is the building blocks of a puppy's life. The DNA profile is unique to the puppy and his entire profile is known as his genome. The genome cannot be changed so once a puppy's genome is set through meiosis, that's it, his genetic traits and materials are all in place. Now, and this is an extremely important bit of information, the genome cannot be changed but there is something very specific that dictates how the dog's genetic inheritance is expressed, called the epigenome.

The epigenome is like a switch that sits above the genome and adapts the dog's wellbeing to their immediate environment. That environment includes things happening inside or outside the dog, so it can include food or scary experiences, amongst many other things. The epigenome switches the gene expression on and off depending on the environment that the dog is in. This is most important when we consider that a puppy is conceived and weaned in a stressful and scary situation to a stressed and desperate mother.

When a mother lives in a scary world, whilst her puppies are growing inside her, her own body is flooded with stress chemicals. Cortisol and adrenaline are heavy within her body and screaming to the rest of her system that she's not safe. Stress causes general body functions to slow down. So, her immune system might not be working – if she is undernourished and bred from in her first season, the nutrients she needs strong bones and organs will go into her puppies and she will not herself develop into a strong dog.

I believe from her health and behaviour that Holly was born in the puppy farm. She's a surprisingly small Yorkie and when she arrived with us her muscles were wasted, and body bent in the strangest ways, with no muscle or weight on her, we could sell Holly's hip joints working. The hip joint in dogs is based on a ball and socket movement and hers seemed to move completely around the joint.

In these pictures Holly had only been with us for a few days. She has been clipped extremely short; through necessity, by her rescuer and when she arrived her hair was starting to grow back. Her ears had no hair on and were leathery and black. As you can probably see by the top picture, her front legs are splayed outwards with little strong muscle between her leg and body.

Holly's back legs were again missing the muscle mass that exercise would provide, In the lower picture you can see that. Her spine was lowered in the middle like she still has a lot of weight in her stomach area. She had also lost her tail; it's likely that she chewed it off or it became infected.

There are other reasons I think she was born in the farm. She has a serious grass contact allergy, so if she walks on grass she itches, particularly in the summer. Her senses are patchy, she can't determine where a sound is coming from, and her eyesight is poor. When a dog grows up in a dark place – particularly if they have limited resources such as nutrition – their body develops what it thinks they need for that environment. So, if Holly grew up in the dark, which I believe she did, she would develop limited eyesight, simply because there was no use for it in her current environment. In the same way, her hearing would not develop naturally based on the acoustics of a farm environment.

As you can imagine when all this is happening in a mother's body, puppies developing within it are going to be at a disadvantage from the start. The stress hormones that reach them through the placenta throughout pregnancy will be warning their bodies about the dangerous, limited, and scary world they are about to enter. Their systems are literally developing with the aim of being ready to run from the danger that they will experience after they are born.

When a devoted dog breeder decides on a pregnancy the health of both parent dogs is assessed in great detail. If there are risks, the pregnancy doesn't happen. Even when there are no obvious risks at all, the genetic throwback from many generations can lead to a puppy with health problems, but the responsible breeder will take every single precaution to avoid this. The veterinarian is consulted every step of the way, much like a human pregnancy and maternity specialists. The mother dog is given the best possible diet, supplements are introduced so her body gets everything it needs to sustain her and the growing puppies. She's kept at home, stress free and comfortable. Vitamins are added to her already excellent diet and only then does the breeder decide the dog is ready to be a mom.

As a total opposite, puppy farm parents are given enough food to stay alive and keep breeding. The farmers spend as little as possible on food, avoid veterinary care, and generally put no money into parent dogs. The aim of this activity is profit. Farmers keep male dogs too, and their escape is not quite so common but occurs. Male dogs are kept in cages in the same way, then released only to breed.

Nutrition is fuel for growing dogs. Nutrients fuel the cells of body, bones, organs, and systems. Without nutrients the dog would die. When puppies are conceived all possible nutrients go into their development, leaving the mother dog lacking in everything she needs to stay healthy. The body is resilient though and the farmers know this. Yet puppies still don't get everything they need, because the poor mother dog is giving everything she has but it still isn't enough. The lack of nutrients in the puppies – added to a lack of any genetic aware and veterinary input – will lead to puppies who look great at six weeks old but are likely to develop all sorts of health problems later on. And the mother left behind to have the next litter will be unhealthier than ever.

The puppies we see on classifieds are likely to be farmed dogs. If an advertiser supplies many breeds, this too is an indicator that they are farmed. There are other signs that puppies for sale are being provided through ruthless methods. They can include lack of interest in the home being offered, cheaper puppies than if they were being bought from a reputable breeder, signs of ill health, lack of veterinary paperwork, and puppies being sold from a website with the use of stock photographs and no presence of the parents.

It's important too to remember that farmers know that people ask questions. I once visited a home where there were two puppies for sale and the woman selling them said that the mother had been sent to her daughters for some peace. I suspect they were a host family ready to take a cut from the puppy farmer, for becoming a third-party seller. Pet shops are third party sellers, too. They take the puppies from farmers and set them up in rooms ready for potential buyers. The public then go in and visit/buy puppies, and because so many people are big hearted even when they suspect the sinister background, feel they need to 'rescue' the farmed dog. They buy the young dog and naturally supply the demand for more farmed puppies.

I'm sincerely sorry if the beginning of this book seems depressing. It's important that we know the basic details of puppy farming along with the origin story of most puppy farm escapees, though, and whilst there are a lot of harsh facts about this topic, we will now move onto the wonder of watching our escapees develop into the dogs they were always meant to be.

Chapter Two:
Man's Best Friend

"When the Man waked up he said, 'What is Wild Dog doing here?' And the Woman said, 'His name is not Wild Dog any more, but the First Friend, because he will be our friend for always and always and always.' "
—Rudyard Kipling

When I saw Lacy for the first time, she was being introduced on an online forum used for rehoming rescue dogs. Her first pictures showed a battered and bruised tiny dog and her description read, "Lacy looks like she has had a sad little life so far," which indeed she did. Aged approximately five, Lacy was picked up in Tipperary by a family who gave her four baths, then she went to Cottage Rescue in Ireland, finally coming across to Friends of the animals in Wales, which is where she was when I fetched her.

We had to piece what we believed her life experience to be together by her behaviour and physical appearance. She had obviously had lots of puppies, her teeth were all broken, her ribs had been broken and healed oddly making her body feel like a few spanners in a pillowcase. Her front legs were bent. Little tiny Lacy with love became cheery, humorous, sparky Lacy Locket and stayed with me for many years. I remember the first time her eyes sparkled, a few weeks after she arrived; it was like someone had opened dark curtains and allowed in the most beautiful ray of sunshine.

I was Lacy's only person for a few years and she gave me everything she had. Finally finding someone she learned she could trust, Lacy opened her heart totally and utterly. She was an absolute delight. When we met my now husband, it took her not quite so long to accept him as her person, too. She had practiced on me.

The little dog that became Racy Lacy had been badly hurt, abused and exploited but she was still ready to love given half a chance. That's because dogs love people; we have a heart connection with them and anyone who shows a dog, in a language they understand, that they can be trusted will win the heart of that dog.

The human and dog relationship is more than special. It can't be described really in words, not in the way that it's felt. Whilst we have likely theories, we can't be sure how we joined. So, I'm going to explain this using the most commonly accepted theory used today.

The grey wolf and domestic dog have a common ancestor. The ancestor liked the waste that humans provided in our early ramshackle communities so started hanging around. They might also have liked us in general at that point, which is something we will never know.

This animal who is no more because he continued to evolve became the animals we know today, the dog and wolf. It seems that dogs, even before they became dogs, had specific personalities (only a few thousand years before we actually accepted that) because the bolder ones joined us more frequently whilst the more worried animals continued their natural evolution into today's grey wolf. At this point we were all still on our evolutionary journey (and of course we all still are).

As far as we know, the animal that became the dog entered a period of relaxed selection, which we fuelled with our own plentiful resources and waste. Relaxed selection is the term given to a breeding boom in population because life is safe, and food is easy to get, humans are doing it right now in fact. Next, because relaxed selection probably led to relaxed behaviour around people we may have got involved in their lives, too. They likely became our hunting partners, guards, and friends. Then we decided who bred with who, because we wanted the fastest, strongest, and most robust canid help, thus began artificial selection.

Fast forward to today and speedily passed a 19th Century breeding boom where artificial selection hit its all time high, and we have over 450 dog breeds all genetically designed for a specific role. You can't change one thing about a genetic animal though without changing others. So, whilst the wild canid went through this process his appearance changed dramatically – sometimes on purpose and other times as a side effect of trying to strengthen another trait.

Some common examples of this are silver foxes. Bred for biddability, they became black and white over a few generations. Collies bred from two Merle parents (which is forbidden by the kennel club) are often born deaf or blind. Completely white dogs have an excess of the "piebald gene" making them likely to be deaf. These ride-along genes are common enough to be a risk and the reason why there are many genetic health problems in dogs bred today.

Despite our meddling and fiddling, dogs are born with a predisposition to being our friends and family. They want a person sometimes even more than they want each other, dogs have evolved in human homes for so long now that they seem to be part of us and us part of them. If you're a rescuer or have been involved in rescue you will know this first-hand. Even the most traumatised dogs want human contact; even if they only ever trust one person, they so desperately want to trust that person.

The Study of Dogs

Over the generations we have studied dogs in many ways. Some studies are ones that should never be repeated again, and we will examine their findings as gently as possible where necessary throughout the book. Lately though we have become way more ethical in our studies and observations; we have become ethologists and increasingly interested in the bond between dogs and people.

Ethology is one of the greatest study discoveries of all time. In the past we captured animals and studied them in captivity, assuming they would act the same as they do in their natural habitats – which obviously they don't. Now though we realise that to fully understand animals we need to sit quietly on the fringes of their natural environments and watch them without interference. To see this in action we only need to watch anything by Sir David Attenborough, who is a wonderful biologist and ethologist, and has bought much of the best wild animal footage into our homes, enhancing our lives, understanding greatly.

One of the most famous studies associated with dogs has also become one of the most unfortunate and still influences the wellbeing of our domestic dogs today. Captive wolves were studied by Rudolph Schenkel in the 1940's and his findings were put forth in a theory of dominance and hierarchy.

Where the wolves were unrelated and fenced in, they simply didn't get on. They squabbled and fought. We know now that this behaviour occurred purely because they were unrelated and as far removed from their natural environment as it was possible to be. Wolves are naturally family animals and their pack is their tribe. Peace is kept by the parents and the family work together as a close-knit team of survival, relationships, and co-operation. Back then though Schenkel believed that his team and himself had made a ground-breaking discovery; wolves all wanted to lead the pack and would do anything for that top spot. This was added to scientific journals and later revoked by the wiser David Mech and yet is still quoted as fact today by people who like the theory and haven't caught up on the last few decades of research.

Ethology and the domestic dog go hand in paw. This is because after many generations of being an integral part of family life, the dog's natural environment is at home with their people and often other dogs or animals, too. So, you can be an ethologist as can I and we don't have to do anything different, just observe and learn. Which is also where we are getting much more accurate information about dogs from, too.

Recent studies are telling us all sorts of interesting facts about our relationship with dogs, and their bonds with us. For example, a dog and bonded human share the experience of Oxytocin when we make eye contact, which has only so far been discovered in mothers and their young. Other findings include dogs whose emotional brain areas light up at the sound or sight of their bonded human and that women prefer to sleep with their dog than their partner as their dog facilitates a much more restful night's sleep.

Now that we have an idea about the strength of our bond, let's take a look at how to communicate intent to our friends in a way they can truly understand.

Getting to Know You

When we saw Holly (then Shelly – they are all given rescue names as in the farm they are just numbers) on the rescue website, I wasn't sure how she would cope with the dogs we already had. With prior knowledge I knew that puppy farm mother dogs were keen to fit in and never really wanted to be any trouble, so I already knew she would be a good little dog. What I wasn't sure about was how she would cope with the noisy gaggle we already had. I called her foster carer at the time and asked. Her foster mom replied that she's a very strong character and would probably join in.

When Holly arrived, she hid her face all the time. As if by not seeing us, we wouldn't be able to see her. There was a dark film over her eyes and she held herself carefully, moved slowly. She was trying to be invisible. This changed as time went by, in tiny increments.

I honestly believe that Holly became the confident – and somewhat demanding – dog that she did because she was given the space to heal without pressure. It's so hard not to try and make them feel better, not to interact, touch comfort, and even cuddle these scared little ladies, but in all honesty if you give into the urge to do that in the beginning, you are likely to scare them. Depending on the type of place they have been living in, puppy farm escapees will usually like and understand other dogs. They have been surrounded by dogs all their life and despite the desperation about people and their plight amongst us they may have dog friends. For this reason, it's usually an excellent idea to bring a puppy farm escapee into a home where there is already another dog, preferably one with some confidence and certainly with trust in people in the home.

We fetched Holly by taking our three other dogs on a 150-mile round trip to visit her. The first sight of her was a tiny little face staring out from behind a sofa and on the way home she sat in a crate on the back seat, just looking at me; she's stared ever since. Her foster carer was absolutely right, Holly was resilient and quite a bold dog underneath the harsh years. She was undoubtedly broken in the beginning though and her eyes were blank, dark, and lacked all the lustre that any little dog's eyes should be gleaming with.

This is the first picture I took of Holly at home. I remember my husband saying that she "made him sad" simply because she looked so broken. She hid inside herself for a long time before she felt secure. Her fosterer was absolutely right, though; where other dogs were concerned Holly new her rights. Because she was itchy, she learned that if she stood by one of them and scratched herself enthusiastically, they would move, and she would get their warm spot.

Holly blossomed because we basically ignored her until she was ready to get emotionally and physically close to us, then when we asked for it, we offered gentle, restrained

interaction. Just like other dogs who have learned proper social skills – in fact as ours did most of the time – we left her to her safe space and let her just tag along when she was ready.

We often see a dog and want to interact, any dog, and this is because the hormone Oxytocin makes us feel affectionate and want to share that affection with the one who triggered it, the cute animal in front of us. Without knowing how that dog is feeling, though, through enlightened observation, we are having a one-sided conversation that probably only we are enjoying. One of the quickest ways to build trust in a dog is to ignore them. In every situation we have with a worried dog, we should avoid speaking or looking at them unless they tell us they are ready.

When socially respectful dogs meet, they totally avoid eye contact and never approach a stranger head on. A good, respectful greeting is delivered as a curve; they go directly for the rear end because that's where all the information is held. If one of the socially competent dogs reads the signals of the other properly, and those signals are saying "leave me alone", then the two won't interact at all, which is fine, too, because they have chosen that.

Communication is the key to success when you bring home a new dog that has never achieved a safe bond with the species they innately want to live alongside – us. We want to love them and show them how safe they are and as humans we do that by touch and attention. Yet for farmed dogs, that attention from people in the past has led to pain, fear, and abuse.

Whilst we are focussed on farm escapees, the act of accurately communicating intent is applicable to every dog we meet but particularly important if the dog has never known kindness from people.

Communication between dogs and people began many thousands of years ago, before dogs were dogs and when our own species was still evolving, too. Whilst the dog's closest wild cousin is the wolf, ours are apes. Wolves communicate by subtle looks, movements, eye movement, postures, a small amount of sounds, and general body language. They rarely touch each other unless they are familiar within a trusting relationship and playing, or are enemies and fighting. They live in a family where the parents breed, and the rest of the group are related offspring. Wolves, left alone, live a peaceful existence. Apes however are grabbers, they shout, touch, throw things around and do battle with each other for power and sex.

If we were to put an adult ape and an adult wolf in a room together and shut the door to observe them, their conflicting communication styles would probably lead to trouble. Fast forward to today and (unless we are educated in canine communication) we are still pawing like apes and unsettling the dogs who naturally prefer the hands and eyes off approach still used by the wild wolf. Most dogs cope, some can't and protest, whilst the very scared dogs see all our natural communication attempts as threats to their already shaky safety.

Bringing a scared and often abused dog into our home is a crucial time for trust building. Remember though that dogs build trust by leaving each other alone, and if we don't leave the dog alone in the beginning, we are likely to be scaring them.

The Importance of Just Watching

Holly slept in a crate in the bedroom to begin with. I remember turning the light on in the middle of the night and she was flat on her back, legs in the air and belly up. She wasn't ready to do that in the daytime, but at night in her comfort she became totally relaxed.

In the early days we simply observed her. Not by watching her with obvious focus but with enlightenment and often through the sides of our eyes. Remembering that to this point, she would have associated human focus with probably brutality. We practiced our own ethology and instead of hidden cameras we watched her without obvious focus, which became a very rewarding pastime.

There's something amazing about watching a dog that's come from a bad situation into a kind home. If you get beyond the need to touch and replace it with observation, you will find that it's much more rewarding to watch than interact. That's because the more we interact, the less information we gather. When we focus on what we are doing with the dog we can often miss the magic. This is an unintentional secret – practiced by all excellent dog people – the less we do and assume when interacting or even working with dogs, the better we are at it. The best dog trainers and coaches make sure their sessions are dog-led. The worst dog trainers crowd, rush, push, and project what they want onto the dog, often leaving her confused and intimidated.

With observation it's important to practice enlightenment. Dogs speak in tiny signals; something may flit across their facial expression for a moment or two. There may be a subtle change in the eye shape or ear position, easily missed unless you're practicing enlightened observation. The signs and signals telling us how a dog feels run into their hundreds and, in many cases, as a species, we can barely recognise ten or twenty of them.

Because dogs are all different and have a variety of face shapes, ears, eye shapes and body shapes it can be easy to misunderstand one breed even when you understand another. Even dogs find it difficult to read the body language of their own species when their shape has been changed dramatically through artificial selection. Creation of breeds has changed the ability to communicate, yet there is still a baseline of communication running below the genetic alterations.

There are many ways that a dog communicates, from tension to facial expression, height of tail, to which direction they are looking in. Dogs that have been through trauma, though, struggle with communication because it hasn't really worked for them in the past, so they stop trying. When Holly first came to us, she was a scared, stiff little dog that you could do anything with. The lady who came to the house loved her, she was so easy and sweet to handle. In fact, Holly made it onto the advertising for the groomer and even in that picture she looked worried.

At the basis of any communication attempt is an inner state. Try to imagine the way that how you feel affects how you act. For example, if a driver speeds past you whilst walking on a country lane you might swear and offer a fitting hand gesture. Your own behaviour is in response to your heightened heart rate, and your internal stress response. In this situation it's likely to manifest as annoyance and indignance – but it's based on fear for your life.

People and dogs (along with every animal that has a central nervous system) have a default fight, flight, and freeze behaviour when we feel threatened. Flight means get out of there, fight is conflict and face the scary thing head on (with the idea of winning), and freeze means wait it out and hope to be invisible. Dogs that are confident and happy when faced with a threat will most often take flight, they may default to fight if they are on a lead and can't escape – often with a display that wants to chase the scary thing away. Yet dogs who have been helpless in their fate will usually just freeze.

A farmed dog has most often been helpless in their fate. This response is not unique to them though and any dog that has suffered at the hands of a trainer, other human, or even animal may default to freeze because they have learned that they are helpless.

Learned helplessness is an emotional shut-down. It's often also a physical and psychological shut-down and it is based on the idea that "it won't work anyway so why would I try" or even "the harder I try the worse it gets". When these dogs come into our homes, they will often appear like Holly did. They will hide their face, move slowly, and try not to be noticed. They will often carry out self-soothing behaviours, too.

Self-soothing may include excessive licking, chewing, digging a bed, or any general signs of stress such as a long, slow lip lick, shaking like they are wet or yawning when not tired. Just as we chew our nails or hair when self-soothing, or we might fiddle our thumbs or fingers, dogs that have learned to self-soothe have their habits, too.

 It took Holly a couple of weeks of emotional freedom before she started to shake off the state of learned helplessness. She was quick and lucky to get from under it so well. I sometimes wonder what she thought of the two huge humans that were so gentle with her. Particularly after learning that people were pretty brutal for so many years. She took tiny choices to test out her new world, the choices that became bigger ones and helped her to finally start to relax. She began to wake every day and tenaciously celebrate that she was still with us. Holly became a six-year-old puppy and started to unashamedly dance into her days.

Chapter Three:
Early Communication

"Because of the dog's joyfulness, our own is increased. It is no small gift. It is not the least reason why we should honour as love the dog of our own life, and the dog down the street, and all the dogs not yet born" –Mary Oliver

It's three am in our house and Holly has woken me three times already. She has managed to get all the blankets off her bed and is trying to scrape them back on. It sounds like she's trying to scrape her way straight off the planet. Before that she decided she wanted to play with a peacefully sleeping Chips, who growls like a grizzly bear when asking to be left alone, which she blatantly ignores, waggling her tiny body at him anyway. Now she's on the sofa in my office, snoring like a train.

Holly's communication is now built in confidence – at home at least. She's still scared outdoors and likely always will be. Yet Holly at home is a miniature ruler and a formidable dictator – far from the dog she once was. She demand barks, pushes the other dogs around, and generally tells us all what to do.

Communication with a dog who has escaped from trauma takes a specific path. Imagine that the state of emotional learned helplessness is a suitcase, packed up tight and the zip pulled around it. It's been packed up for so long that even if we unzip the case, the contents don't move, so we have to gently tease them out, one at a time. This is similar to the way a dog with learned helplessness begins to communicate.

Canine communication is a big topic. It's fascinating and especially so when we see it developing in a dog who is trying tiny new behaviours, because she is in a space safe enough that she can. Seeing those little attempts and signals is one of the most rewarding things you will ever do. These tiny steps are exactly why people get addicted to rescuing ex-breeding dogs and have a gaggle of them around their ankles at all times.

Dogs are born with the natural ability to communicate with each other; they practice that ability with their siblings and mother whilst they are being whelped and learning to play. At the beginning they are helpless little suckling machines, with closed ears and wobbly bodies. Even the puppy's brain is barely developed at birth. They do have a very special nose, though, which is heat-seeking and helps them find their mother and food source. So, if they are moved away from mother, they wriggle back on that fat little belly, to eat or sleep next to the most important thing in their tiny world – their mom.

As they reach two-weeks-old they become a little more animated. As the weeks pass, they become little play blobs, they start to use communication skills after only a few short weeks on earth. Puppy play is clumsy. Play is based on ritualised behaviour, fighting, biting, wrestling, and eventually (when they can move quickly enough) chasing. It's carried out for fun and the aim is to maintain the play; for that the puppies need to be good communicators. If one puppy bites too hard when playing, one of two things will happen. Their partner will reprimand them, and the game will end. This is the point that puppies learn to inhibit how hard they bite. In a process called bite inhibition. Bite inhibition is the act of learning only to bite hard enough that is needed to maintain the game, which ideally translates later in the puppy's life to biting hard enough to be left alone by the scary thing.

Canine communication is intricately associated with social learning. A dog who was born in a puppy farm like Holly may be an excellent communicator with other dogs, particularly if she shared a pen with them. When dogs have no positive contact with humans, though, they don't learn that we are safe, and they can't communicate with us at all.

Social learning for dogs is a weakness we have created in the Western world. We often have a family dog, bring them home as a puppy and treat them like an extension of the human household, as opposed to the dog that they are. We naturally hinder their social learning from other dogs – often with the best intention. In addition to this, unless we learn dog language, we literally isolate the dog because they are not exposed to anyone they can naturally communicate in their own language with. These dogs adapt; there's no species so adaptable as the dog after all, but we have to ask ourselves if that's fair to them.

The dog's brain develops as he grows. That little blob of jelly present in his tiny head when he was born starts to form pathways, ideas and beliefs about the world. Imagine it like a blank (ish – because some behaviours are genetic) state that is developing electrical charges through it that will be strong enough to dictate how the dog feels, acts, and reacts for the fifteen or so years they are on this earth with us.

There are a couple of surges in development as the puppy grows and these are even more important for social learning. If learning doesn't take place on one subject during the first few months of a puppy's life, the dog is likely to struggle with it later. Some common examples of this are the couple who get a puppy and never introduce their dog to children, but five years later have a baby. Or the well-meaning dog owner that picks their puppy up to keep him safe and doesn't understand why at six months old the puppy can't suddenly be relaxed around other dogs.

In Holly's case and the case of most farmed dogs, particularly if they were born in the farm, their brain is good with dogs, but everything else is a terrifying enigma to them. They can communicate with dogs but when approached by a human, they only experience fear.

Holly's suitcase was packed so tight that she must have been under the impression that she had no choices at all. When she was picked up, she went stiff. When touched she waited it out and she attempted very little communication in the beginning. She started to show herself, though, and we began to see the following common attempts at communication gradually be tried and tested.

Whilst I describe these signs as communication attempts, they are also general behaviours. Any behaviour is a sign of a changed emotional state. For example, a dog who looks scared is likely experiencing a fear reaction and the dog that goes stiff as a sign of learned helplessness is likely to be shut inside themselves. To notice any changes in the dog's inner state, we only need to learn what those changes look like on the outside.

I'm going to use a comparative example here, just for the sake of understanding. So, here's my disclaimer – this is intended as analogy, not anthropomorphism. Not that I mind a bit of anthropomorphism anyway, as Marc Bekoff says, "It's OK to be anthropomorphic, it's natural to do so, and critics are wrong to say we should never do it" (Canine Confidential published 2018).

Take a moment and ask yourself what it feels like to be totally neutral. You might be neutral now, as you're reading this. Or you may have some kind of emotion going on. You could even be a little irked at my recent embrace of anthropomorphism, or you might even be relieved by it. Neutrality is hard for humans because we have an extremely active mind. It's always chattering on about something, and in comparison, no-one knows what the dog's mind is doing other than the dog. Ask yourself now, what you look like on the outside when you're feeling neutral. It might take a little while, because often we don't see ourselves; have a think about it anyway, when you have no strong emotion going on, what do you look like? What little behaviours or shapes do your face and body make?

Next ask yourself how your neutral look changes if you experience a strong emotion. If you become annoyed, how do you look on the outside? What does your face do? Do your muscles tense up and is it visible? What about when you're sad? Does your face drop or screw up to try and stop tears? Or when you're happy, does your entire face and body relax?

Knowing yourself in this way will help you to better understand what your dog or dogs you meet are experiencing, or how they are reacting to you and other things in their environment. Every dog has a neutral stance and we know tried and tested signs of how they feel through much capable ethology (learning by watching). By learning the science of communication, and observing neutrally your dog, you will know when they change on the inside, because they will show you on the outside.

Observation

Observation is your key to fully understanding your dog. So often people bypass observation and jump straight into interaction. Yet the more we observe (and the less we crowd) the new little life that's joined us as a scared dog, the quicker that little life will blossom.

What are you looking for?

You're looking for signs of a neutral and changed state. With the information we have available we can learn what those signs look like, with accuracy, so let's take a look.

All communication and body language should be viewed with the whole dog and the context in mind. So, we consider not only how the dog looks but also what in the environment could be affecting how they feel.

We start at the dog's nose and read all the signs to their tail, which should give us a good idea of their inner state. We then apply what we have learned to the dog's immediate environment and we should get a good idea of the direct contributors to that state. Remember genetic influence over how a dog looks, when you're working out how they feel. First of all, teach yourself your dog's neutral position. This is usually a relaxed state: the face is soft, and eyes are generally soft, too. There's nothing in this dog's environment that triggers any strong emotion in your dog at this point. Her ears will be in the default position for her breed and so will her tail, her body posture will be neutral and usually quite relaxed. Holly is showing a neutral position here. This was her first Christmas Eve with us; she's literally asking what we are doing next.

An important thing to remember is that a dog who has finally escaped from a puppy farm or other long-term traumatic situation may initially have tension as their neutral stance. Yet with their personal growth and their journey into relaxation that will change. How long it takes will depend on the dog. From neutral a dog will either get happier and more relaxed, playful or stressed and fearful. Signs of being happier and more relaxed will include further relaxation,

soft muscles, soft eyes, and maybe even a genuine smile if we are lucky. A smile from a dog is not a toothy display like it is for people as in dog language that means something very different indeed. A dog smile is a wide mouth turned up at the edges and looks like the image shown here. Here's Penny, smiling all over her pretty little face.

Holly doesn't smile like Penny is above, yet she does in her own way. Her little stumpy tail lifts and wags, usually before she starts demand barking for play and she has a surprisingly deep bark. In this picture Holly is full of mischief. Look at her bright eyes! She's almost certainly going to start telling me what to do, any second now!

With a new dog who has lived through trauma, we are initially more likely to see worry, fear, and anxiety than we are happiness and relaxation. All dogs will eventually relax if their environment allows it. They may not totally relax like a dog who has known only kindness, but they will start to feel secure if we facilitate that for them. It's important that we know the signs of fear and worry. This empowers us to ask what is triggering that fear in the moment and how we can change the trigger, to help the dog.

Triggers

A trigger is anything that may change a dog's behaviour by changing the way that dog feels. Most often described with fear and stress in mind, trigger identification is key to understanding.

The image below shows this in action. In the case of a scared or traumatised dog, anything can be a trigger. From a passing child, like in the picture, to a fly by patter in the home. For dogs that have learned people are dangerous and brutal, simply looking in their direction can be a trigger for crippling stress and fear.

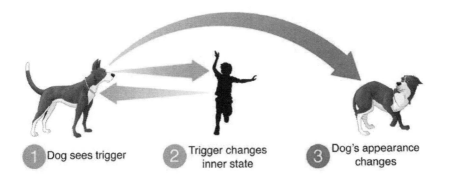

| 1 Dog sees trigger | 2 Trigger changes inner state | 3 Dog's appearance changes |

The most important thing to remember here is that your dog decides her triggers. Whilst we might think a gentle stroke should be comforting and certainly not a threat, it's not up to us to decide what the dog sees as a threat. The dog will decide, often subconsciously, and we must follow their lead.

Internal Affairs

Every mammal has an internal survival mechanism. In fact, we have many but the one that seems to go astray in puppy farm dogs, or simply dogs suffering with stress is the nervous system, specifically the fight, flight or freeze reaction. One division of the nervous system is always working, it has many important jobs including keeping the dog alive by helping her to deal with or escape danger.

If the dog interprets something as dangerous her body begins to change on the inside. Without conscious thought her brain fills with cortisol and her muscles are drenched in adrenaline. The body takes on a 'mind' of its own here and the dog becomes a passenger of the physiological changes that are occurring. The body decides that digestion is not necessary because what good is food if the threat kills you; it also switches hormonal output and regulation to lower significance, and the immune system steps down to make way for all the changes the dog will need to escape. All of this is going on by the time we see external changes, particularly if we haven't learned the micro signs of stress. Another interesting thing is that when this happens the pupils actually dilate, so the dog's eyes look different. which is a massive clue towards what's going on inside.

These highly efficient internal affairs are wonderfully effective and have kept the dog alive for thousands of years. They have been central to survival and success of the canine species, keeping them alive to pass on their strong genes and making them as common on earth as we are. The problem is, though, that when experienced sometimes, the stress reaction helps, but when experienced all the time it can cause a lot of problems – because no-one benefits from stress all the time. In fact, not only is it a chronic illness in people it also affects our dogs.

The dog's stress reaction is something that if experienced once a week or even better once a month can be overcome. It can take up to 72 hours to get over a stressful experience and for all the aforementioned systems to return to normal, healthy function. Yet if a dog, for example my little Holly, has stress as part of her life for the entirety of it, things in her body are going to start to go wrong. When an immune system is switched off, hormones are awry, and digestion is messed up by constant fear or stress, the body doesn't function properly. For example, digestion doesn't get the food to the cells, so the bones might develop a bit bent or her immune system is low, so she may suffer with allergies.

Good Stress

Stress doesn't always have to be negative. After a dog feels secure in their home some short bursts of stress can help with learning short-term positive stress, called eustress. Eustress is the reason we perform better under a deadline and the reason that our dogs learn so effectively in that point between enthusiasm and overwhelm. This stress can be carefully triggered by a good canine coach, with motivation and observation. For example, a dog may be learning something new and getting ever more excited for the reward, so their stress system helps them by releasing some extra cortisol. This gives them a spurt of mental energy and BOOM they get the idea.

Whilst confident and happy dogs will often benefit from this carefully managed coaching session with an excellent coach, who is both aware of dog body language and the tiny signals of overwhelm, our farmed or fearful dogs may take some time to get there. Our initial aim is to reduce stress in their lives altogether, so we just need to be their quiet and trustworthy safe space.

The signs that a dog is starting to feel uncomfortable are pretty universal; even if they can't naturally communicate with us, they will still display signs of unease that we can read. In fact, even complete learned helplessness has symptoms. If we know what to look for, we are empowered to help.

Signs of Stress

Stress is shown in levels. Low level stress is more likely to reverse when we read it and back off. As the level of stress heads towards overwhelming stress though, the dog is more likely not to recover quickly, so will suffer from the reaction for lot longer (up to 72 hours depending on how severe the stress gets). Our job as the lucky guardian of such a delicate friend is to read the earliest signs possible, then change the trigger, to prevent the dog's stress reaction from getting more severe.

Early signs may include the following, which I have structured into loose groups including what the dog is likely to be trying to tell us.

"I'm not sure about what's happening here"

Licking their lips or nose. A dog with learned helplessness often licks their lips with a wide and slow tongue. Most dogs lick their faces or lips if they are feeling uneasy. Sneezing or snuffling might show the presence of stress, more often when the dog is feeling conflicted and this can be seen most often when the dog is learning or playing, often as a symptom of eustress. (The good stress that aids learning). This behaviour can also be shown by a happy dog, resulting in the appearance of laughter.

Yawning when the dog is approached, not tired, or in a situation change can tell us that the change is making them uneasy. Tension around the lips and eyes may show the onset of fear and stress. The tension is something that is extremely subtle, and you might really need to look for it. Pinched lips are a sign that a dog is worried. "I'm not sure about this new thing happening."

"Please leave me alone"

A lowered head or head dip occurs when the dog's head goes below the line along the dog's back. A head dip is a subtle sign whilst a lowered tail when the dog feels uncomfortable will always be lower than their neutral position. A dog that has escaped from a puppy farm may take a long time to raise their tail, which makes it all the more rewarding when they do. A tucked tail and body might be accompanied by a paw lift, which is used in a few situations. It can accompany stress and worry through general unease or be a signal of appeasement.

A slightly changed ear position, ears that go out to the side of the head, even by a little bit, may show appeasement feelings. Ears that go backwards may be telling us that the dog is scared. A dog with long or heavy ears, for example a Cocker Spaniel, may pinch them into the side of her head.

Averting their eyes away from the thing that worries them, including you. The dog who averts their eyes may also turn their head away. Head turning, looking away, and ignoring are displayed in a way that almost appears like the dog thinks if she can't see the stressor, it is not there. This behaviour can be an important sign of low-level stress but is also common in the state of learned helplessness. Some dogs will look at the wall to avoid being looked at.

Eye narrowing and blinking are signs that a stress reaction might be starting. She may also show a dilated pupil depending on how quickly she is getting stressed.

"I'm busy, please go away"

Sniffing in this context is a type of conflicted behaviour. The dog can see the stressor but decides to *change the subject* instead. The act of intense sniffing is another way for a dog to give the impression of ignoring the stressor in the hope that it goes away. This is not to be confused with a dog's natural need to sniff and explore with his nose, as scent is the dog's way of exploring his world; sniffing enriches his life greatly. By exploring the entire dog's body language and the situation in context you will be able to recognise what type of sniffing the dog is displaying.

Vocalisation accompanies body language to give a bigger picture of how the dog is feeling. Some dogs are naturally vocal and whine whilst excited, or anxious. Their exact state can be determined by considering their entire stance and position, along with the external context. It's important to note that farmed or abused dogs might be silent to start with – as they have spent their lives trying not to be noticed.

Shaking off occurs when a dog has passed through mild stress and is returning to a neutral state. We often see this when a harness or collar is removed or when an anxious dog comes through their own front door after a walk outside. A shake off appears like the dog is shaking water from their coat, as opposed to shivering which is a sign of severe fear or illness.

Whilst I have given you the simplest explanation of dog requests and language, you might not actually see many of them in the beginning, particularly if your new friend is suffering with learned helplessness. A lifetime of fear or even a session or two with someone rough can leave a dog thinking that any choice they make will make things worse for them. They stop trying and just wait it out.

Holly is very much a dog who arrived that way. Even a few professionals – including the vet – have commented on what a good dog she is to be handled. The reality is, she's learned that any protests mean it gets worse for her. (That said, no more than ten minutes ago she growled a deep growl because Chips, our tenacious boy, was trying to lick her eyes. Twice in well over two years I have heard Holly growl, she simply doesn't. But it's early and she's snuggled so she made that choice, leaving Chips looking a bit surprised to say the least).

Chapter Four:
The First Few Weeks

*"Before you get a dog, you can't quite
imagine what living with one might be
like; afterward, you can't imagine living
any other way.* –Caroline Knapp

During my days in the Royal Army Veterinary Corps there
was a phrase thrown around regularly, "Prior Preparation
Prevents P*** Poor Performance". It was all about
organisation, being ready and thus as a result excelling in
your performance. I was completely hopeless at military (but
that's another story).

The preparation required for bringing home a puppy farm
escapee or other scared dog is 20% physical and 80%
mental/emotional on our part. For example, we need to
make sure they can't escape, as these dogs will run. We also
need to make sure that there is a little armour on our hearts,

and that we have plenty of patience, puppy pads, and enzymatic cleaner. We simply can't place any importance on our carpets.

Kindness and gentle communication will always prevail in the end. Remember, though, in the beginning that an escaped puppy farm dog is highly likely to have suffered greatly at the hands of humans, and by default we are a scary, scary species. Often, they have never been in a home, they likely don't know the luxury of a dog bed, and their little paws and legs will have spent their lives so far on a wire mesh or urine-soaked hard floor. Providing an easily accessible bed and letting the little dog know what we expect will take a few weeks of communication in a language they understand, and often another dog to show them the ropes.

The Value of Social Learning

Whilst we can do everything possible to show a worried dog that they are safe now, we are not dogs. Our language towards them will be clunky in comparison to a confident member of their own species. A confident dog will teach all kinds of positive things, simply leading by example. It's well known and well-studied that dogs learn from each other, we call it vicarious or social learning.

Many rescues state that a puppy farm dog must go to a house where there is another, confident dog living there. The other dogs certainly helped Holly when she arrived, even though they became a gaggle of animals that barely acknowledged her advances and determination to play. They went outside for a pee, so did she. They enjoyed contact and affection from us and before a few months were out, she was shouldering between us and them to get her fair share. Without the other dogs Holly would have found it much harder to learn how to live with us. She probably never had a human scratch her (now plump) little rump before she came to us. Now she races up and does a final twist, she loves it.

All the basic things about living in a house can be learned by a new dog, from another dog already in situ. It might take a while, but it certainly softens the blow for a scared dog who find themselves living in a totally unfamiliar world with the species who scares them most of all.

There's a vicarious learning canine coaching technique developed to exploit social learning by dogs from people. The techniques are amazing to watch and try. Designed by Claudia Fugazza, *Do As I Do* Training is based on the studies of dogs that watch and learn not only from other dogs but also from exploring how dogs learn by copying people.

There is a lot of scope for using social and vicarious learning when we bring a scared dog into our homes. Learning by imitation takes away the worried dog's unease about our direct focus. Later on, when she realises that you are her person, this little dog won't be able to get enough of your attention. She will soon be making up for lost time, but initially we need her to feel safe just in your presence, so learning by imitation is fantastic.

Watch out for the neighbours though if you decide that you need to show your new charge how to pee in the garden!

Setting Your Expectations

Setting your expectations is a big part of rescuing any dog, even more so when the dog is not a typical steady, stable, and happy-go-lucky new friend.

I'm actually envious of the journey you are about to share with your new dog. There are only so many dogs we can rescue in one lifetime (particularly when your husband is seriously allergic to them) so my opportunity to see the puppy maker become the puppy is limited. I'm going to share yours, though, so please do send me pictures and stories of your progress as you go! My email address and Facebook page are at the end of the book.

Move like a Sloth

Expect to feel like a big scary monster in the beginning. Your dog is likely to be scared of quick human movement. They might have been handled roughly, kicked or shoved aside whilst their puppies were taken away. The visual experience of a person moving quickly around her is likely to trigger an instinctive reaction of cringing, which in the beginning is common but usually fades. It will make you feel bad, though, but it will settle down. You can minimise the risk and frequency of this type of reaction by moving around your dog, rather than going directly towards her when passing. Moving slowly, talking quietly, and making your movements deliberate will give your friend the extra emotional space she needs. The fewer quick movements and direct approaches she encounters early on in your relationship, the quicker she will settle down and feel safe in the long run.

Consider also that doors can provide quite a challenge for the dog that has experienced them in a puppy farm. This dog may have been shoved through doors or even kicked through them. They may have tried to get out of a pen and been shoved or kicked back in – which will cause a long-term fear. So, if you stand in a doorway and ask her to go through, it could be a terrifying request for her. Back off and turn away, or even better go through first as she will feel much safer behind you than she would standing in front of your feet. Eventually when she learns that you can be trusted, this fear will fade, and she will be much bolder in your company.

Cleaner at the Ready!

Toilet training can be tricky to start with. If you get hung up on your deep pile or woollen rug, you might find the first few weeks a bit stressful. Remember though that this little dog has lived in a pen twenty four hours a day until recently. She had no choice but to eat what was thrown in to her, and toilet where she slept – which all dogs will avoid if they can – so she has some learning to do. My best advice is, roll the rug up and shut the door to your deep pile unless you are present and watching for the smallest signs that the dog needs to go. Signs might include glancing at the door, sniffing the ground, scratching the ground, and expect to miss them because you're looking the other way for a moment, it's all part of the journey.

Puppy pads and a good enzymatic cleaner are a must. Put pads everywhere to start with. Little lady dogs often prefer soft pee places to hard floors because they get less splashback, so if the room has boards or tiles, they will head for a puppy pad, as far away from their new cosy bed as they can get.

Enzymatic cleaner will be your best friend. The difference between that and any other cleaning type is its ability to crystallise urine and diffuse it into the ether. Any area that still smells like a toilet – even if it's your deep pile – will stay a toilet. If you can remove the scent your dog is less likely to go back.

Getting them outside after eating and sleeping is also a good idea. How you do this will depend on their confidence and interest in the outside world, and the weather. If you have more than one dog, they will learn to follow their new friend into the garden and often pee on their pee (if they are that way inclined – which Holly is). If it's just you, though, you might have to start picking them up early on in your relationship, to get them into the garden. When she has been you can drop a few scraps of tasty food for her and open the door back into the house. For confident dogs, this stage might involve much praise and appreciation for their timely watering, but a scared dog will benefit more from a quieter, less overt approach. A simple murmured "good" and a dropped treat in the beginning will suffice – plus of course getting back into the safety of the house is a functional reward of its own.

Sometimes dogs pee because they are worried or anxious (deep joy, I hear you sigh). Leg lifting in boys has many reasons, it's information and self-recognition, it also allows other dogs to recognise them and be aware of their presence. Dogs know their world through a scent picture and, as we well know, urine has a very significant scent. A worried dog might pee all around the boundaries of their home, to keep out intruders and make them feel safe; this can easily include floor length curtains – just in case the scary monsters outside try to climb in! Consider it setting the alarm. Female dogs might urinate from fear. It's an extremely submissive response to stimulus, it's also communication to the other party that this dog is extremely scared and asking to be left alone.

In all honesty it's vitally important not to get hung up on bodily fluids when you rescue dogs. You can minimise the damage with well-timed prompts, but you can never guarantee that the dog won't pee up your curtains, and to get exasperated or stressed about that is likely to affect your good mood more than it should. Get your cleaner out, give it a good scrub, remind yourself that you should have watched more carefully and get on with your life. It's no big deal.

Sometimes people still punish dogs for toileting indoors. Can you imagine how it must feel to be so worried that you pee yourself, or so scared that your only safe space will be invaded by monsters that you need to secure all the boundaries any way that you can – only to be shouted at, threatened or hurt for coping with your fear in the most natural way to you? Even if you're confused about which bits are toilets and which are not, punishment seems extreme doesn't it? We all have to "go" after all. No-one is exempt from the need to pee.

Punishment for any kind of behaviour or choice, towards any dog, is counter-productive to your relationship. It does work, it's also mean and brutal. There's a theory that the punisher simply enjoys delivering punishment which is why they keep doing it. I suspect it's true, along with lack of scientific knowledge on how demoralising and confusing it can feel to be punished. But enough about pee. What else can you expect from your newly rescued puppy farm dog?

Your relationship with your new dog will mature like a fine wine. There's no quick delivery of love from the dog that has learned fear. There is very much an innate need to have a person of their own, though. So, whilst other dogs might be on your lap within minutes, this one may think about looking your way for a fortnight, practice it for another month and eventually take a few steps in your direction by month three of being in your home. Just because they don't show it, though, it certainly doesn't mean that the bond with you isn't building, it will be, quietly and with such conviction behind those wary eyes, that if you could feel it physically, the power would simply blow you away.

Walking

When we took Holly for her first walk, we drove to the centre of a woodland and parked. Making sure there was no-one else around we opened the car doors and the other three dogs raced off in glee. Holly decided she didn't have any legs. Coaxing, begging, chivvying, and encouragement led to carrying and a swift online order of a front carrying dog bag the very same day. Next, we tried the beach and gradually she found those legs and the bag has never been used.

When we consider walking it's important to remember that a puppy farm parent dog may never have seen the outside world. There has been a huge change in their life already, by coming to live in your home, so depending on how keen they are, the rest of the world can wait.

Many dogs don't need to have a walk every day. Some do and benefit greatly from it, for example the dogs bred to do active jobs like collies or spaniels need to go out daily and use up the physical energy we have created within them. Dogs that are stressed by the outside world, though, might be better staying at home more often. Activities at home will be better for the scared dog than any amount of walking, because they will feel safer at home.

Dogs have a myriad of energy needs. Some will happily have a run then settle for the day, some need the opportunity to use their breed related traits, and others will like a short walk yet benefit greatly from mental exercise. Some dogs cope with never going off the grounds of their home, particularly those homes with nice big grounds. When we look at the needs of the dogs we care for, we have to consider their individuality.

The questions to ask yourself when assessing the exercise needs of any dog are:

- Am I building a physical athlete trying to tire my dog but it's not working?
- Am I getting and keeping my dog healthy?

- Do I meet her needs to forage and problem solve as part of my dog's daily routine?
- Do the walks she has fulfil all her needs?
- Does my dog have the right kind of exercise to fulfil the needs she has right now?
- Does she like walks, if not what can I do differently?
- What is my dog's body language telling me about the situation she is in?

It's a bit of a myth that an exhausted dog is a happy one; certainly, they need to meet their physical exercise needs and many dogs love long walks, exploring the world. Long walks in new places are physically and mentally stimulating, so meet a lot of the dog's needs, for dogs that excel with this lifestyle, and of course it's better to walk further than not at all for most dogs. There is something important to remember, though – not all dogs are the same.

When we think that all dogs need to be physically beyond tired, to be truly happy, we also incorporate some habits into their lives, for example the ball launcher, which has the dog running backwards and forwards in a kind of predatory daze, until her tongue lolls and she flakes out. With this type of exercise, we are not only fuelling obsession but also creating more fitness, so the more shuttle runs the dog does – the more she will need to do. In addition, she will still need to use her mental energy regardless because there's not much thinking involved when she runs up and down in straight lines.

Dogs that become stressed by the outside world and are walked through their triggers regularly can suffer with long-term stress which will affect their health and wellbeing. In this case it's good to build your dog's capacity for walks, take it at their pace and choose walk areas carefully. For example, don't walk a dog scared of other dogs at the dog park at the busiest time of day or the dog scared of cars on a short lead alongside a busy road. Both of these approaches will make your dog vulnerable and stressed.

The puppy farm escapee will naturally be worried about the world. The best thing to do with her is use up her energy at home for at least a couple of weeks after she arrives. She will have a lot of decompression to do, so adding a walk in there will adversely affect her lowering stress levels and her growing wellness. Only walk her when you think she is ready and, in the meantime, let her get used to her new life in her own time.

There are some at home exercises that will meet your dog's needs and build her confidence greatly, all of which we will cover in the next chapter.

On A Lead

When you and your dog are ready to face the challenges of the world together it's important that you have physical hold of her. A scared dog is highly likely to run away, fast. Having a lead and collar or harness will prevent any mishaps, any escapes, and a great deal of heartache.

 I always use a harness for walks. The dog's throat is delicate and any pulling on a collar will potentially cause damage and pain. The well-fitting, soft harness is a good way to have control without putting your dog at any risks of throat problems. Choosing a harness is an important job.

Holly had a red, quilted inner fleece one when she arrived because not only did it hold her lead but it also sat around her chest and front part of her tummy area, snug and warm, with the aim of keeping her feeling safe, too. This was suitable for Holly because she's tiny and gentle on the lead. If your dog is stronger and tends to pull, you may need something sturdier.

In my experience a dog will accept a comfortable harness much more easily than they do a collar. Feeling something around our necks when we didn't choose to put it there is enough to make any of us feel insecure. However, the presence of a comfortable harness can soon be overlooked. The best piece of advice I can give you when first trying a harness on your dog is to communicate with her carefully, read how she feels through her behaviour, and use plenty of tasty food. If it takes a few sessions to get it on, that's fine. Remember to look away from her slightly whilst you do it, as this will make her feel more comfortable. When she has it on at home leave it on for a while and then, with no fuss, take it off. The short periods of wearing it will help her get used to the harness in her own time.

Before you take your dog out in her harness check it thoroughly for safety. Fear makes dogs do extreme things and the world can be randomly terrifying for us, never mind a tender little dog, so if there is any chance your dog can slip out of her harness you need to change that.

Introducing a lead will be interesting because a lead makes it necessary for your dog to walk close to human feet, which is scary for puppy farmed dogs, for all the reasons we have already covered. I suggest a long, strong yet light lead that keeps your dog physically connected to you but doesn't restrict their space or pull them in close to your moving feet. I use a flexi lead with Holly. There are only a few situations where a flexi lead can be considered a safe option. For example: when we are walking in fields or open areas away from roads, when the dog is light and doesn't pull and if the benefits of that extra flexibility outweigh the risks of a hand burn courtesy of a fast-moving flexi cord. For Holly, a flexi on the beach was perfect because she could walk with me, safely away from my scary feet and I still had hold of her for security.

Flexi leads really shouldn't be used with collars as the impact of getting to the end of it with speed can damage the throat. They should never be used by roads because they can be erratic and have been the reason for dogs jumping or wandering into moving traffic on many occasions, some leading to fatal consequences.

If you have other dogs, hopefully the new one will see how happy they are on a walk and feel at least a little relaxed. It's important that you watch her carefully for any changes in body language and behaviour that show she's becoming stressed. A good indicator of stress is if you drop a little food and whilst she would usually gobble it up, she's not interested.

Go somewhere quiet initially where you won't be ambushed by people and dogs. You need space to be able to see how your friend is coping, then when you know she's OK you can start to build. There are so many different dogs that come from puppy farms, yours might dance around on her first walk, celebrating. She might be worried or prefer to stay home for a while. It's up to us to try and work out their individual preferences. Some dogs you can let off the lead and practice recall quickly, others need to stay on. Holly went off the lead at around walk four and has been at my ankles since.

Holly's first time off lead at the beach.

Loose Dogs and Fly-By Petters

If your rescue dog is happy with other dogs, which many are, then meeting other dogs on walks will be the least of her worries. They shouldn't be the least of yours though because unfortunately some loose dogs can cause trouble. Just as you are learning to read the body language of your new friend, I suggest you take some time to understand the intentions of others.

The world we live in is awash with dysfunctional dogs, which is sad but true. With little opportunity to learn from well-balanced elders who teach manners to their young friends and family, dogs can become thick-skinned thugs. It's not their fault but their behaviours may include running up and getting in another dog's face repeatedly, jumping in or knocking a dog over, not reading a gentler dog's behaviour, and ignoring natural cut-off signals. All of this can be overwhelming even for the most social dog. Don't get me wrong there are a lot of wonderfully empathetic, kind, and genuinely responsible dog walkers in the world and they are truly a pleasure to meet. It only takes one that isn't, though, to affect the wellbeing of our dogs forever.

Sadly, sometimes people have their dogs off the lead and don't recall them, even when the dog is aggressive towards others. Unfortunately, we can't completely trust people to be thoughtful or sensitive to the needs of our dogs, so we have to be prepared to protect them from stressful experiences on our own. Often these people can't read the intention of the dogs they are with and so simply don't know what their dog's body language means. So, my advice is, learn to understand dog language and yet still be aware that the odd person you meet may be irresponsible enough to put both their dog and yours in danger.

Fly by petters are common, particularly if your dog is small, cute, and frozen with fear. They approach with desperate hands for the touch, assuming that because your dog is quiet and not looking scared, she doesn't mind. From the dog's perspective she has a strange human (remember it's the species that she has learned to fear most) looming over her with a huge advancing hand and super-focussed staring eyes. If this happens to you don't be afraid to stand up for your friend, as she can't do it herself. Try to do it in a way that elevates their understanding, but if you can't don't be too hard on yourself.

If you do what my husband did once and (after his polite requests were ignored a number of times by someone persistently trying to touch a terrified tiny Holly) and you find yourself shouting at someone not to touch anyone or anything who doesn't belong to them, live and learn. Don't blame yourself, we are only human after all. Sometimes being ignored by one more fly by petter is one too many and they become the straw that broke the camel's back, especially when you're in charge of the welfare of a little lady who has suffered years of fear and abuse.

A Note on Expectation

Setting your own expectations for bringing a puppy farm rescue dog home is the most important thing to do. In many ways it's different to bringing a dog home from another environment, yet we do exactly the same thing; we react and respond to their needs. It's just that their needs are special. The first thing I learned from my two saddest ex-breeders is that they have an inner resilience like no other dog, it's just well-hidden. The second thing I have learned is that they seem to intuitively want to fit in without causing too much fuss. These dogs don't want to cause us any trouble and seem to go out of their way to be *what we would consider* good dogs. They just have some necessary unpacking to do along the way.

Chapter Five: Healthcare

"Opening up your life to a dog who needs a home is one of the most fulfilling things you can do. –Emma Kenney

Sometimes when we care for scared dogs, we do things we wouldn't normally do. Holly's homemade haircut is a necessary lesser evil that would be handling from a stranger. Holly wasn't difficult for a groomer; she is actually the perfect client because she freezes and waits things out, but the reason for that freeze is learned helplessness, and that's the point. So now the vet looks at her and momentarily thinks, "Cushing's disease". Let me explain, on checking her over recently he asked about the obvious "thinning of her coat" to which I had to admit very quickly that it wasn't quite thinning that he saw, but my less than professional hair clipping job. We all had a good giggle and the vet asked if I could do his hair, too.

Wellness

Health and care are the basics of rebuilding the physical dog back into the strong little individual she should always have been. Wellness is a holistic process and covers much more than physical health, as everything is linked.

People tend to shy away from the term holistic, thinking that it means avoidance of science. Holistic actually means the whole dog. Biology, emotional wellness, psychological wellness, and social wellbeing are all part of holistic health. In human health we have a term called META health and this is a fantastic term to apply to the wellness of your dog, too.

META health means everything!

So, imagine the veterinarian, diet, social situations, the ability to use up mental and physical energy, the absence of stress and emotional wellbeing are all clustered together, then draw a big ring around them and we can label everything within that ring, META health.

The Veterinarian

A couple of weeks ago we took Holly to the vets for coughing. We took little Rosie too as moral support and all four of us went into the room together. The vet that ushered us in was new to our family, and boy she talked. In place of listening was talking, in place of information gathering was interruption, and by the time we got out of there all four of us were stress panting.

The lesson here is that vets are only people and their skills are personal to them. This means that choosing a vet is important for both you and your dog. It's quite an intense experience for everyone going to the vets anyway, so choose carefully.

Thankfully there are many more vets with skill and empathy in social situations than without. You may already have a veterinarian that has your trust, you may be looking for one. If you're looking for one use crowdsourcing of information by asking people local to you, perhaps ask on Facebook or other social media, and make your decision wisely. Remember that you may go through some tough times around the veterinary surgery you choose, so friendly faces and empathy are a must.

When a dog has lived in a barn or farm, without exercise and on the cheapest possible diet, she will have a long healing process to go through. Things might arise associated with that process, and as she gets stronger, she may need to see the vet regularly.

Itchy Scratchy Dog

From my research and in my experience, itching is common for dogs that leave puppy farms. Holly still itches now and, in the beginning, she was scratching all day and night. Thankfully it's much improved.

The dog's skin is their immune response whilst ours is our respiratory system. Allergic reactions affect the immune system and allergens cause different responses in us. For example, if I were to be exposed to something I'm allergic to regularly, I would get respiratory system problems, such as the inability to breathe, causing swellings in my nose or a runny nose. The dog however will get itchy skin if they are regularly exposed to allergens, they may even get hot spots.

If your dog is itchy over the first few days of being home, it's a good idea to check for parasites. If she came through a rescue she should already have been treated. If not, she may have fleas or even mites which are causing her itching; if her ears are itching, she might even have ear mites which come with a smelly ear, presence of black tar, and lots of frustrated scratching. If there are parasites present, you may need to get her a treatment from the vet to rid her of them.

Unfortunately, parasite treatments through extreme chemical routes can be harsh towards the dog's health. Whilst she is healing your dog could probably do well without chemical treatments but sometimes they are necessary for a definite infestation. There are many types of parasite treatment available from the vet. If your dog has fleas, I suggest you carry out some careful research and ask assertively which is the least invasive and use that one, as many are coming under scrutiny for being harmful to dogs. If your dog doesn't have parasites, perhaps consider more natural preventatives.

Natural flea preventatives include diatomaceous earth which are tiny shards that are harmless to the dog but if combed through the coat, destroy the outer skeletal form of fleas, killing them through dehydration. The food grade diatomaceous earth can be added to their meals, as a preventative measure against worms.

Breeding dogs for looks, which most puppy farms do, will negatively affect their natural hardiness. Immune systems are less able to come and often their endocrine systems are also flawed by the time they get into the world (which is not only the case for puppy farm parents but the puppies themselves). Whilst all the systems within the body can be affected by many different chemical changes, the immune system can become overwhelmed. Another thing we can keep in mind is the effect of stress chemicals on the immune system, which we are increasingly finding out, and can often cause a natural immune response.

Other reasons for itching may be food quality, airborne allergies, contact allergies, and chemicals both in the diet and environment. Finding the exact reason for itching can be a challenge. Sometimes if the dog has had a vet check it's a good idea to wait it out, to see if the itching ceases as your new dog regains good health. It may drive you a bit mad for a while but could settle down now your dog's diet and environment is healthier for her.

Often the first step for veterinary treatment for itchiness will include steroids or other drugs. Whilst steroids give instant relief, they often only supress the symptoms, which makes the dog more comfortable in the short-term. Sometimes steroids are prescribed long-term. The trick is that they are given at the dose the dog needs, for only as long as they need them, which is the vet's task.

Vaccinations

Puppy farmed dogs are often not vaccinated whilst in the farm. If they are retrieved by an organised rescue, they will receive their full vaccinations at that point. So, when they arrive with you it should be done. An initial vaccination is important because a dog who has lived all her life in a puppy farm will have low immunity. Her body will not have been exposed to the dangerous virus cells that she can encounter in the world.

Vaccinations are coming under scrutiny for their effects on dog health, however in the beginning a first set of vaccinations is (in my opinion) the lesser of two potential evils. It is likely to tire her immune system, but the initial vaccination is important protection for a dog who has not yet been out in the world. After the initial vaccination you have more of a choice. This will be a year into your life with your dog and you can have her immunity checked via a simple blood test known as a titre test. The results will show you whether she needs a vaccination in her second year with you.

All physical illness, changes and worries about your dog should be checked out by her veterinarian. It's a legal stipulation that only qualified veterinarians can diagnose, treat, and prescribe medication to animals. It's an excellent idea to look at the wellness of your dog through the META model but always involve your vet if you consider she may be unwell.

Food

As you will be feeding your dog from the moment she arrives, it's important to remember that her meals will have been small and sparse to this point, yet because she's been hungry for most of her life you will want to give her a decent-sized meal. Beware though because it's easy to overload a dog that has a shrunken stomach, by wanting them to feel satisfied, in a process that will lead to inevitable diarrhoea. It's a good idea to split her meals carefully between six a day than gradually bring them back to two as her stomach gets used to eating well.

Stress can cause stomach upsets, too. So, you may want to choose easily digested food that's gentle on digestion, for example chicken or white fish and rice for the first few days, just to keep the food bland enough not to irritate the digestive system as your dog settles in. Any changes to diet should also be done gradually by introduction of new food in small quantities over a few days. This is particularly important for a dog that has been on the same food type all her life as sudden changes can also affect the tender digestive system.

Choosing a Food

Dog food is big business and can be incredibly confusing, here I'll attempt to dispel some of the fog. Until now, your little puppy farm escapee is likely to have eaten dry kibble with very few nutrients. This might show in the shape of her body and her general condition.

Food is vital to health. In fact, I would go so far as to say that it holds full central position to wellness because it literally fuels the cells that build your dog's tissues, organs and systems. Good food fuels strong cells that are able to regenerate and support excellent health whilst poor food does much less – in fact in many cases it keeps the dog alive but also floods their bodies with chemicals.

Dog food began to change when we decided to make the act of feeding our dogs an easier process, while remaining certain all their nutritional needs were met at every point in their lives. When we became completely responsible for feeding our dogs, and began turning them into pets, we created dog food.

Over the last couple of decades, pet food has become a big profit product for manufacturers. The dog food that we buy in packets, tins, and sachets with a long shelf life, barely resembles food at all and is far removed from the whole-food source that it once was. Canine convenience food has, on a dog's health, the same effect that eating tinned, dried, processed, and additive-filled ingredients has on ours. Dog food may contain certain vitamins and cover her basic nutritional needs; most canine convenience foods do that, but it could also contain chemicals that act as poison in her healing body.

Some of the most common dog foods that we buy, even the ones that are sold as individually-owned, small manufactured meals, are owned by huge corporations. These are often profiteers that spend more money on marketing than they do on quality. Most dog food manufacturers lay claim to having our dog's health in mind, that each of their ingredients is hand-picked and that they sell only the very best.

There is no independent governing body that regulates dog food. This means that no-one is checking whether the food that we provide for our dogs is good for them. Everyone that checks the quality of dog food has a financial interest in the food selling and selling well.

One of the most important things to learn is how to read ingredients and composition labels on dog food. Not only for you but for any clients that you may work with, in an advisory role. The labels on pet food, particularly the supermarket brands, are complicated and it is easy to skip passed them rather than look up what the scientific word for each ingredient means. Take some time looking at the food that you are currently feeding your dog and ask yourself how close to actual food some of the ingredients are.

The meat source is listed first, often described as some kind of 'meat meal'. Next is the fat source, followed by the filler. The label ends with the long chemical names for flavourings and preservatives and finally any botanicals and vitamins that are added. Some dog food packages have a listed composition of over fifty ingredients. Yet quality meat, calcium, carbohydrates, and suitable plant matter are good, whole, natural foods for dogs.

Chemicals, colours and preservatives from food will labour a dog's body. The chemicals in many traditional dog foods have an adverse effect on their health. In addition to flooding the body with chemicals, when we feed standard commercial dog food, we are also not providing the quality meat and vegetable matter for the dog's body to thrive.

There are no enzymes, fresh vitamins or fresh foods at all in a daily bowl of kibble.

Diet options are split into three groups. Commercial food, home cooked, and raw food. Each have their positive points. A good, simple, home-cooked fresh whole food diet made from organic ingredients is going to provide the best nutrition for your dog. This food can also be supplemented with a carefully selected kibble or wet food to increase available variety. Another option is to provide an entirely fresh, raw diet that can be supplemented with vitamin and mineral powders. The third choice is a good quality commercial dog food, created with health and nutrition as its core value (you can confirm a food's suitability by carefully reading the labels). If you choose commercial food it's a good idea to add fresh vegetables and meats in as often as possible, to get an excellent range of vitamins and enzymes into your dog's healing body.

Eating Superstitions

When your dog arrives with you, she may have some funny habits around eating. These are often gathered as superstitions and may not make any sense at first glance. For example, a puppy farm dog may never have eaten from a bowl, instead having food scattered around their messy pen so they had to gather it up. The sound of a bowl touching the floor may make them jump, causing a superstition. Often puppy farm dogs won't take food from the palm of our hand, or sometimes even our hands at all. This is unsurprising because they my see hands as grabbers; along with our feet they are the most dangerous bits of us. We will discuss hands later in the book, but for now, don't push or rush – remember she needs time to heal.

My Dog Won't Eat!

There are several reasons for a dog not eating. Along with superstitions there may be health issues, tooth issues, or digestion problems. If your dog is eating, then stops, it's worth getting her checked over with the vet.

The Importance of Clean Teeth

Holly only has a few teeth, she arrived with them and manages fine, despite them having the somewhat unsettling appearance of a tiny abandoned Victorian cemetery.

Dental problems are common with small dogs and particularly when they have not been properly cared for early in their lives. It's thought that build-up of plaque in the dog's mouth can affect their organs and general health. Often when a dog already has a significant amount of plaque, the vet might perform a descaling operation under sedation or general anaesthetic which takes all the plaque away along with any unhelpful teeth leaving us with the responsibility of keeping those teeth nice and clean in future. This is something we can do by building trust and using enzymatic toothpaste if we can. If we can't do that, good chews will help with tooth cleaning. Twenty minutes of chewing a day is thought to keep teeth nice and clean.

Choosing chews is as complex as choosing food. Rawhide has a terrifying creation process and is actually developed and tanned as an offcut of leather, so is best avoided. Many dental chews have a wide range of chemicals in them. So, it's vital to read the ingredients carefully. As we have learned so much about the sinister side of dog food, many manufacturers have started offering excellent quality chews, alongside top-quality commercial food. Many people feed raw or cooked bones to their dogs, which is a personal choice for you. Choose them carefully, though, as bones can splinter, getting stuck in the intestine which calls for an emergency operation to save the dog's life. Raw feeders use carefully selected bone types, such as chicken wings. If you're thinking of feeding a raw diet it's important to do lots of research on balance, bones, and generally meeting the dog's nutritional needs.

Joint Care

When a dog has not walked far into their adulthood, their muscles will be weak and soft. Muscles and the muscular system - specifically the skeletal muscles - have the important task of maintaining the structure and shape of the joints.

As I mentioned earlier in the book, when Holly arrived with us her joints were not supported by her muscles at all. She was a funny little combination of angles and bends, when ideally her joints will have been strong, and her muscles toned enough to hold them in place.

With her funny angles and lack of physical strength in mind, we walked Holly on short, careful walks to begin with then built her up to strengthen those muscles so that they could naturally offer more support to her joints. Muscular support is amazing; any muscle can be built in order to take pressure off joints. It must be done carefully, though, and alongside excellent nutrition/supplementation for an overall support system.

Joints are a little different and rely on both muscles and nutritional support to stay strong and healthy. The dog's joints are also affected by genetic inheritance so if a parent dog has joint problems, her puppies can inherit them too. This is a topic that has much debate around it because many experts believe that nutrition is far more important than genetic inheritance on joint welfare. Like all nature or nurture topics, the truth is we really don't know where one begins and the other ends. We do know that nutrition is extremely important to health which gives us something real to work with.

When people breed from dogs with welfare in mind, they will check the joints of these dogs first. This is done via information gathering and even x-ray techniques. A dog with problems will not be bred from. As you can probably imagine, puppy farmers don't check yet still breed. When we bring a dog home from a puppy farm, even if there is no obvious long-term joint issues other than muscle wastage, it's a great idea to provide joint support anyway, because if we keep putting in the right vitamins and supplements, the joints have enough nutrients to stay healthy, for as long as possible. Often, we can wait until something goes wrong then go to the vet because our dogs are in obvious pain; early bespoke supplementation may help prevent that, in some cases for years.

The structure of a joint depends on the joint itself. The hips are ball and sockets, whilst the front legs and knees act like levers. Within the joint is a small amount of fluid that keeps it supple and skeletal muscles are attached with tendons. As all dogs age, their joints will show some signs of wear and tear, just as ours do. When a dog is healthy, fed well, and grew up being well looked after with careful exercise routines, the joint will naturally be stronger for longer. When an adult dog escapes from a puppy farm and is a bit rickety, we have to start where we are and support her at this point moving forwards. Thankfully we have access to a lot of knowledge and possibilities for slowing down joint problems and helping our dogs.

Walking too far too soon is going to put excessive strain on joints that don't have much muscle mass, so it's a case of taking things steadily and building distance gradually. Muscles will become stronger the more they are used but dodgy joints need strong muscles before we ask our dogs to walk too far.

There are two types of joint problem, osteoarthritis and joint dysplasia. The first occurs through general wear and tear, whilst the second can be a pre-existing condition exacerbated by a number of factors, including injury, poor nutrition, or genetics. Nutrition is important for joint wellness; specific supplements and vitamins designed for support of the joints will help. There are hundreds of joint supplements available for dogs, and it is difficult deciding which one is best for yours.

Common good quality joint supplement ingredients include:

- Chondroitin Sulphate: A natural component of cartilage. This helps to reduce inflammation and prevent further damage in the joint.
- Glucosamine Sulphate: Widely used in human joint supplements. This helps to rebuild damaged cartilage and acts as a natural anti-inflammatory agent.
- MSM (Methylsulfonylmethane): This acts as an antioxidant and anti-inflammatory.
- Omega 3 & 6: Essential fatty acids are necessary building blocks within the body. They help to repair damage within the affected joints.

- Green Lipped Mussel: Studies have shown this is effective in helping to reduce joint pain, swelling, and stiffness.

Joint supplements can be an easy and safe way of helping to protect your dog's joints. It is also important to remember the importance of a good quality, balanced diet, maintaining an ideal weight and providing sufficient exercise to keep your dog's joints healthy!

As we work through the book, we will continue to look at wellness in a more hands on approach. Sometimes healthcare needs to be coached with positive and careful methods in a form of fear free husbandry, which is why I'm saving grooming and checking for the section where we begin actively teaching through kind positive reinforcement.

Chapter Six: Fear

"Dogs are a really amazing eye opener for us humans because their lives are compressed into such a short period, so we can see them go from puppyhood to adolescence to strong adulthood and then into their sunset years in 10 to 12 years. It really drives home the point of how finite all our lives are"–John Grogan

When Holly had lived with us for over a year she had started to really come out of her shell. She was extremely confident in the house and glad to meet other dogs on walks; her fear didn't include other dogs at all. Things were going great for her, but then it went wrong.

We were walking at our local park and an older man had four dogs off lead in the area. One of them, a female terrier, was out with two of her puppies. The mother came towards

Holly and silently, viciously attacked her. With a scuffle we got the dog off and got her to the vets, where she went straight into surgery. Fortunately, the physical wounds healed but sadly the emotional ones have scarred.

Because the only thing that Holly wasn't really scared of gave her (what is likely to have been) the most terrifying experience of her life, she has developed a strong fear of unknown dogs. The attack affected our whole family. Soon after it happened, we started getting outwardly annoyed at people allowing their dogs off lead to approach us. The adrenaline linked to the approach of an unknown dog turned to anger, based on sadness that we hadn't been able to keep our tiny dog safe. We had gained a strong, learned fear that had affected all of us, in one single traumatic event.

Fear is one of the strongest and most primal emotions a dog can experience. It can be so strong that one single event will burn it into the neural pathways of their brain and keep it there as a default response every time something similar to that single event occurs. The scientific term for this is one trial or single event leaning, meaning that if something is traumatic enough, the dog can be scared of that situation or similar one – for the rest of their lives.

There are things we can do to help them. We may be able to lessen the impact of the fear by teaching new things, new associations and understanding. Or they may always have that fear, it depends on the dog and severity of their experience.

Neural Pathways

The dog's brain and nervous system is made up of neurons, which is the name given to those specific nerve cells. Neurons speak to each other via a process of electrical charge, referred to as the synapse. There are also different types of chemical that we call neurotransmitters. When our dogs learn something new, a new route through the neurons is taken - the route then leads to a final decision. It often takes a few practices for the neural pathway to become the default route leading to that specific decision, yet with severe stress or fear, it may only take one.

A good analogy for understanding neural pathway routes is the garden that has become overgrown. Imagine that you have been dropped into the middle of a walled garden, which is a square patch of unruly grass with four tall walls. On each of the walls is a gate and you have to choose which gate you want to go through, then get there by treading down the grass to create a decent pathway. Just the act of treading down the tall grass has made this a slightly easier route. So next time you get to choose which door to go to, and one of the paths is easiest, because you have already trod it down. If you follow the same route ten times there will only be one actual route in that garden, so that's going to be easiest one for you to take. It will become your habitual route, eventually the only choice you make.

This is pretty much how our dogs learn to repeat their choices, how we form habits, and how the brain works in general when we are making decisions. If we then imagine driving along to one of the gates on a ride-on powerful lawnmower or even a rotavator – churning up the ground as we go. That's how quickly a neural pathway is established when the dog gets extremely scared.

One trial learning isn't the only reason for fear, though. There are a few, and for a dog born and bred from in a puppy farm, it's more common than not. Dogs can suffer with fear, phobias, anxiety, and obsessive compulsions. There is an area in the dog's brain (and in the human brain) called the amygdala. Directly associated with the fear response this is the part of the brain associated with learning to be scared. The reason for the fear is usually something interpreted as danger or a threat.

Important note: the dog always decides the threat, and whilst the response may seem exaggerated to us, for the dog the danger is very real. Therefore, we must respect how they feel about something and help them.

When the dog is scared their inner state changes quickly and severely. Fear and stress go hand in paw and whilst stress is the physical response to a stimulus, learned fear can trigger that stress response even when the dog is not in any danger. Just like some people may have a phobia of harmless mice, that causes their heart to race, palms to sweat and the need to get away from the tiny explorer, a dog may develop a fear and concern about anything at all and to that dog the fear is overpowering.

It can be quite difficult to recognise fear in a puppy farm escapee because of learned helplessness. These little dogs have for so long been in a situation where they are very scared but also not trying to draw attention to themselves that they simply freeze. The untrained eye sees a calm dog, whilst the trained eye sees a helpless one.

Another example of learned helplessness we might see is a dog who started off confident but a little unruly, trained with brute force and ignorance, for example by an electric collar, the dog may be confused, anxious or downright scared but anything he does to try and alleviate how he feels results in a shock, so he just stands still and waits it out. The trainer may claim victory, but again to the trained eye, it's emotionally shut dogs. The dog has given up trying.

The Appearance of Fear

Fear has a varied appearance and exactly how we see it depends on the dog. There are four dogs in my home, and they all show fear differently. Chips barks at the scary thing, constantly, looking as ferocious as he possibly can. Vinny spook barks, in a tirade of noise that flows from one bark to the next deafening everyone in his wake. He also height seeks if I'm near, climbing and clawing me. Rosie drops her Pomeranian tail and Holly waits it out. Since her attack Holly has started taking flight when scared, which is a different choice but no less worrying.

How your dog deals with something scary will be an individual process. If they currently freeze, like Holly does, it may change as they unpack. Let's take a look at some common ways that dogs deal with fear.

Hiding

Hiding within herself is Holly's default fear response. Scientifically known as freeze she will tuck her rear under, avert her face and hope for the best. This response is characterised by stiffness, avoidance, yet an inner belief that they can't get away. Wide tongue, slow lip licking is often shown as an involuntary action.

Running

Trying to run away is the flight response in action. This may be a default for some puppy farm escapees. Characterised by low body language, and speedy retreat, taking flight is a natural way that a dog will respond to danger if she has the choice.

Going into Battle

Dogs won't often choose to fight, because it contradicts survival. Wild wolves usually sort out their minor and even some major differences via negotiation because to fight means they get hurt which will naturally weaken the entire pack. Dogs too will not fight if they can help it. We do however inadvertently encourage the fight reaction in them by exposing them to scary things without giving them the chance to escape – for example we have them on a lead and make them stay close to the thing they fear. When this happens to a dog, they lose their option for natural flight and in its place they try to chase the scary thing away. This is the dog's natural fight response and why we see them barking and lunging so often. It's a behaviour that shouts, "Don't come by me I'm dangerous" but actually means, "I'm scared and must look scary, too".

Body Language

The body language of fear will be presented as either tucking in or puffing up.

We see tucking in with hiding, freezing, and non-confrontational fear. The dog's tail will pop underneath and her rear end might tuck, too. She will pull her ears back (or pinch them if they are heavy). She might show some signs of stress such as licking her lips and trying to hide behind her person's legs or other barriers. This dog just wants to be left alone.

Puffing up occurs when the dog is open to battle to defend herself (or is trying to give the impression that she will be a tough adversary). She will probably make a lot of noise, the hackles rising along her back and base of the tail. Puffing up doesn't necessarily mean this dog is aggressive, just that she's learned this behaviour works by sending the scary thing away, or simply that she's learned this neural pathway soothes her in this situation. We don't often see puffing up in farmed dogs because they have so often learned that it doesn't work or gets them into trouble.

The exact response of any individual dog will be based on their own individuality and, with your dog, it's a good idea to watch them carefully for the early signs that they might be scared, then get them out of the situation that's scaring them.

Safe Distance

Distance control empowers the dog and it empowers us if we understand it and use it properly. The ability to control how close our dogs get to something and increase the space between them, and that potentially scary thing will build trust in our dogs, teaching them that we have their backs. Keeping things at a distance where our dog feels safe, and increasing the distance if we need to, shows our dog that we will do everything we can to keep her safe.

Dogs use distance control as part of their natural communication with each other and with us. They have three definite distances within which they can feel safe. The social distance, flight distance, and finally the critical distance.

 Social distance means how close she feels comfortable to others in her peer group. Holly's social distance is tiny; she would love to curl up with the other dogs, but their social distance is not as comfortable as hers. She manages it, though, and often they just deal with her persistence.

The longer that Holly has been with us, the happier she has become in her social distance to us, as the humans that she first feared. Underneath her rough start Holly is a determined, resilient extrovert. She and I had a conversation just last night where she was totally determined to sit closer to me than any other dog whilst we watched the television. As I told her to settle down, I saw something in her eyes, a defiance and determination that both amused and warmed my heart. She was having that place on the sofa. By hook or by crook that spot had Holly's name on it and in no uncertain terms she told me so.

There are certain cut-off signals a dog will offer to another dog or person if they don't want to interact. A common one is looking away, her ears might shift position slightly, moving only a tiny bit to each side of her head. She might lick her lips or look into the distance. If you are ever approaching your dog and she does these things, she's asking for space and to adhere to her requests will build her trust in you.

The next distance is more serious and known as flight distance. Try to imagine an invisible bubble around your dog. When she's in the bubble and all other things are outside it, she's safe but if the walls to the bubble are breached – particularly by something she finds scary – her stress reaction will begin. Despite it being called flight distance, the dog will always default to their natural flight, freeze, or fight response when their safe space within the bubble is breached.

This is where we are empowered to help our scared dog because we can learn the size of their safety bubble and ensure, as much as possible, that nothing scary penetrates it. This will help her to relax and builds the confidence she so desperately needs. Look out for changes in her outer appearance and body language, work out what could have triggered the change, then get her out of there. If you increase the distance between your dog and the trigger her safety bubble will return to being intact.

If a dog is not able to get away or is forced into the presence of a trigger, she will soon reach her critical distance. For a dog without learned helplessness, this might be shown by a terrified freeze. For a dog with the confidence to use aggression, she is at risk of biting. The critical distance is the point where the dog feels that their life is truly in danger. If the critical distance is breached, the full-on stress reaction occurs, which takes up to 72 hours to dissipate.

Fear Aggression

An aggressive response will not be relevant for all dogs. Remember that learned helplessness takes away all possible options for the dog, so she may believe that aggression doesn't actually work for her. However, it's important to consider it because all dogs are individuals with individual responses.

Fear aggression is one of the strongest and most severe types of aggression because a dog suffering with it may believe that their safety and even life is at risk.

The dog that shows fear aggression will often show a conflicting response to a trigger; they may back up, avoid the trigger or look away, their body might show a flight response, or a mixture of fight or flight which seems contradictory, for example a display of all teeth but a tucked tail and body. The dog showing fear aggression is keener to give a warning than to actually bite, but she will bite if the worrying thing continues to advance or won't leave her alone. The physiological experience a dog is having when she shows fear aggression is severe. Her stress reaction is in full force, heart rate raises, breathing increases, shakes, trembles, and may urinate or express her anal glands.

Dealing with Fear

When fear is learned, it can usually to an extent be changed or at least lessened in its severity to help the dog. Every behaviour needs to be observed and understood before we can consider changing it, simply because we need to know what's going on for the dog, to ensure we are working on the correct problem.

If your own dog is experiencing fear, beyond what she can cope with and it's not getting incrementally better as she settles outside the puppy farm and in her now safe home, it might be a good idea to find a positive, empathetic, and kind professional to help you understand why. If you have trouble finding someone, email me (contact details are at the end of the book) and I'll help, because there are a lot of worrying dog trainers in the world who can do much harm to a scared dog.

In a professional role we can deal with fear in a number of ways and the exact approach will depend on the dog. For example, a dog with general anxiety may need a very different approach to one who has learned to fear people or other dogs but is relaxed otherwise. To understand fear, we must again take a holistic approach. This will include understanding what triggers the fear, what maintains it, how intense the fear is, how it has developed and whether the dog needs veterinary help.

If you have rescued a puppy farm dog, I can guarantee you it will be a couple of years before you stop seeing fearful responses, if at all. So, don't expect her to relax overnight or think that there is something very wrong if she doesn't improve at the speed of light. Remember she has many years of sadness, so it could take a couple of years for her to fully unpack. You will however be rewarded with amazing little glimmers of hope and happiness along the way. I remember Holly's first few weeks with us and how I would leave her in her bed in the bedroom, then she would wake up in her own time then literally dance into the room. Just like she was celebrating that she had woken to another day of good fortune. Now she's keen to lie in every day, I don't know if she's forgotten how she used to wake up in the puppy farm or simply realised that this is her life now.

Dealing with fear professionally involves identification of it, then a careful mixture of coaching techniques to help the dog to cope. The approach may involve medication if the dog is suffering with generalised anxiety alongside her fear, a condition that can only be diagnosed and treated by the vet and will be a short-term solution that should be used alongside coaching and behaviour help. There are also a number of complimentary supplements, approaches, and therapy types which can be highly effective.

Behaviour Therapy

Behaviour therapy for fear towards triggers can include counter-conditioning and systematic desensitisation and should always avoid flooding.

Counter-conditioning means that we teach the dog that the trigger of their fear means something else, something nice. Conditioning is the word given to learning, counter-conditioning means that we counteract that learning with learning something more useful, it's usually carried out alongside systematic desensitisation and can work really well. To work properly, this approach is carried out at a point the dog is under threshold because if her stress reaction starts, it will not work. The basis of this learning process is that the dog sees something that was scary and learns that the presence of it means something nice. In neural pathway terms, the dog sees that a different gate has a favourable option, so instead of heading along his usual path to fear, he starts treading another path – to the gate with the tasty treats.

Counter-conditioning can go wrong if it's not taught by a scientific professional, who can recognise when the dog is reaching her threshold but can be extremely effective if it is taught responsibly and with empathy.

Systematic Desensitisation is dog led and is the act of bringing a dog and trigger closer together gradually whilst the dog is calm. It basically makes the safety bubble smaller and the dog more able to cope with things in her immediate environment. When used with counter-conditioning, the two together will usually work well. Think of it like this: the dog sees a trigger and gets a treat. The trigger comes a bit closer and the dog gets a treat. The dog is given time to relax and the trigger comes a bit closer, the dog gets a treat, and so on. The real trick is to keep this going over a few sessions whilst also keeping the dog relaxed. If her behaviour changes, the process has been moved on too quickly, if she stops taking the treat she's probably stressed because the trigger is in her safe space. This dual technique needs a sharp trainer eye to prevent flooding.

Flooding is often carried out unintentionally. It means that we expose the dog to the scary trigger or situation and expect her to just get used to it. The idea behind flooding is that the dog (or human, because it was used on humans too for a long time) can't maintain a state of high stress or fear for a prolonged period so just gives up and naturally copes with the trigger. Now we know that flooding doesn't help, in fact it leads to learned helplessness, so it should not be used with dogs or people. Unfortunately, when someone can't actually identify learned helplessness, they assume it means that the dog is suddenly coping, when really that assumption couldn't actually be further from the truth.

Remedies and Therapies

Complimentary remedies and therapies have come a very long way in the last few years. As the wellness of our dogs has become central to their care, many complimentary approaches that have been used for a long time are being offered by people who have seen them work with their own dogs, so want to help others.

Supplementation of herbs, flower remedies, and nutraceuticals are commonly available, giving us plenty of choices and even a little confusion, because there are so many available. The individuality of dogs dictates what will work for them.

Remedies may include emotional healing through Dr Bach's range of flower remedies. Flowers and floral remedies have been used as natural medicines alongside herbs and spices for many years. Flower remedies are usually prepared as a liquid solution that is administered via a dropper or pipette for oral use. Flower remedies may also be mixed in tiny amounts with drinking water.

In the 1930's a bacteriologist and pathologist, Edward Bach, personally developed a collection of remedies, made from naturally growing flowers. His research of natural flower remedies was a direct response to his own poor health. Following surgery to remove a tumour in 1917, Edward Bach had been given the news that he had only 3 months to live. With his remaining time, he decided to dedicate his life to the study of flowers and their medicinal properties. It was 20 years before Bach passed away, one year after completing his life's work. The result of this work was a collection of 38 remedies, made from naturally growing flowers, each created to heal a specific emotional problem. Though scientists cannot specify exactly how, each of these remedies work perfectly to restore natural and emotional balance to the individual.

Probably the most commonly used flower remedies to come from this group is rescue remedy. Rescue remedy is designed specifically to target anxiety. Used by people and the owners of anxious dogs to calm their pets, rescue remedy is one of the most popular natural anxiety remedies available.

Herbs that have been shown to calm down stress and anxiety and sometimes vitamin therapy or nutraceuticals will help. Ideally if you would like to explore remedies further, you will be able to identify a holistic veterinarian to help with choice and suitability for your dog.

Touch therapies can be a little more difficult for dogs that are not comfortable with human hands on them. Although TTouch is a great technique for confidence building, and it's well worth learning.

Tellington TTouch was developed by Linda Tellington Jones in the 1980's. Tellington TTouch is internationally recognized and constantly evolving to produce a forward-thinking approach to handling, training, and rehabilitating dogs (amongst other animals). TTouch is a therapy all on its own and developed for animals that have behaviour problems, unrest, or emotional disharmony. This therapy type was developed for use alongside a positive approach to dog training. The idea with TTouch is that we go at the dog's pace, touching only when they are happy and in the style that they are happy with, to restore holistic balance to the dog. It's a fantastic, none-invasive practice that you can see working as your dog relaxes into it.

Chapter Seven: Confidence Building

"Curiosity will conquer fear even more than bravery will" –James Stephens

I have learned that Holly is an extrovert who has been trapped in learned helplessness for too long. She loves people and when she knows them will actually demand bark for attention, then swing around offering a plump rump for a rub. There are only a small handful of people who she meets, but she certainly remembers them and is getting braver with new people all the time, when in her own home. She's also recently started thinking about taking food from my plate, whilst I'm actually eating it. A very brave dog indeed.

I celebrate every achievement on her part, even when she's telling me what to do, in a bark that would better suit a Labrador, or dancing around my office because she believes three pm is way too late for me to still be working – despite the fact that I want to. If you're a dog *owner* who likes rules, or you expect a dog to be seen and not heard, show respect to the humans as their pack leader, or expect them to act like obedient robots, you would hate this home.

It's chaos in this house and the chaos is largely to do with the conduct of the dogs, with Holly right in the middle inciting riots that she might in some way benefit from and she usually does, and there's (unintentional) positive reinforcement in a nutshell.

Empowerment Through Choice

Part of the reason I believe we are seeing Holly's true self is the way her confidence grows through regular problem solving. I also think that the freedom she has to try things out help her to try more all the time. Choices are so vitally important to our dogs and in fact they have very few, we chose them after all, they didn't choose us. Even when we offer them a happy home with plenty of love, they still have few choices.

Think about the freedom we have as people. We might think we are stuck for a multitude of reasons; money, relationships, people, or necessity all give us the impression that we have little choice. On a wider scale, government, taxes, and world politics allow sinister beliefs to grow, beliefs that tell us that we are stuck, when really, 99% of the time we are not. We have options. We can study, change jobs, change relationships, move home, or even move to another country if we want to. Yet our minds have given us the illusion of lack of choice.

Dogs, on the other hand, do have little choice, particularly in the UK and other countries where they are heavily "owned" by people. Dogs can't move home, change their daily routine, decide what we buy them to eat, go out for a walk when they feel like it, or decide they are fed up of an abusive relationship (if they find themselves in one) and leave. Dogs are pretty much at our mercy. In addition to this we have for so long been taught that any freedom of thinking or behaviour from them represents dominance and must be met with further boundaries, even punishment.

Thankfully things are changing. People are starting to recognise that it's okay for a dog to show sparkle. The term obedience is being cast out with the demons and replaced with life skills and manners. We are beginning to stop issuing commands and instead teaching cues, through positive lessons, games, and dogs are being encouraged to be themselves. In amongst all this positive change is a practice of learning and living through choices, which makes my heart sing.

The real key to facilitating choice for our dogs, in a way that works, is to facilitate the right choices which make their conduct and behaviour acceptable, yet still allows them to be themselves. There's no point encouraging choices that create awkward behaviour or a tense home to live in. That would cause frustration and that's simply not the point. We will discuss this in more detail in the next chapter, when we talk about kind and clever canine coaching, but for now let's look at problem solving.

Last year we had a fantastic dog sitter stay with the dogs for a couple of weeks. One of her shocked comments on our return really made me laugh. She pointed at Holly and said, "She's mad for food". She really is. Holly has been hungry in her life, probably for many years of it. When she first arrived, she would snatch an unfortunate passing spider, if we were not quick enough to intervene, and gobble it up. Now, I'm pleased to say, she's a bit more discerning than that.

We have used and channelled that desire for food into some really excellent confidence building activities and it's worked really well for her. The other dogs love it, too. I'm pretty sure that Holly would rather find her food hidden in boxes and toys than be given it in a bowl.

Problem solving for food is excellent for dogs that are scared of people. Building confidence without having to interact with a human – in the beginning – is the first step towards actually having the confidence to build a direct relationship with us. Think of times you have solved problems. How did you feel afterwards? Did you experience a little glimmer of new self-belief? Did you feel like you could take on something else new afterwards? This is what problem solving does for dogs who are scared of people.

Temptations to Avoid

You have probably seen the practice of offering a scared dog food from the hand, to associate that food with us as a pleasurable thing. It's what we do, based on the idea of passing them some nice food to let them know we are friendly. It might even be another evolved habit from our ape ancestors. When a dog is really scared, though, an outstretched hand, even with food in it, is enough to set their stress reaction off. The associated vocal encouragement and the fact we are watching our dog to see what she will do is scary too.

There is another risk factor to handing your worried dog tempting food, even if she comes towards you to take that food because it's so tasty, she may suddenly realise that she's closer to a human hand than is wise and panic then, backing off with fear and another new association about human hands being really scary things.

Another thing we see – often through Facebook videos – which can be well-meaning but is misguided, is the glove on a stick ritual. I find this practice odd and watching it be carried out on a dog is quite distressing. The dog is usually squashed up a barrier like a solid kennel wall and someone has a glove on a broom handle stroking them gently. In this situation the dog is giving so many signals to increase distance and unless the dog needs medical treatment, I can see no reason for touching a dog that's this scared, this early in the process.

The key to building trust with a very scared dog is not to be looking at them, but to be looking in the same direction as them, and this is why problem-solving activities are so very effective.

Problem Solving

If your dog is anything like Holly you might be able to advance to quite complicated problems quickly. Or perhaps you should start smaller and simpler; if your dog's self-belief has taken a bashing by life this is a good idea. For the rest of this chapter we will go through a range of problems, for a range of different dog personalities, so there should be something for everyone.

Foraging is one of the most natural behaviours for our dogs. Puppy farm dogs may have spent a lot of time hungry and may even have eaten insects that they could catch, which is a form of finding food where they can. The domestic dog became our companion based on his ability to forage and eat from our waste foods, and it's a skill they have practiced for many thousands of years since.

Scattering

Soft sniffing is a genuine way to build confidence without the complexity of hard or noisy things that may make your dog jump. The basis of sniffing for tasty food through or within something soft is tiring and fulfilling. In the summer and assuming your dog has no allergies, the soft, dry grass is a good place to scatter food. If your dog is very low in confidence, just drop a little bit of food on short grass to begin with and build up to more food in a bigger area. You might want to invest in something extremely smelly for this; wet, tiny, and tempting foods will let off a lot of scent. For example, grated goat's cheese or finely chopped liver.

Indoors you can do something similar with an old towel without having to spend a fortune. Just drop the towel flat on the ground, allow your dog to watch you pop a few bits of food onto it and then fold it once and move away from the towel. It's a good idea to sit on the ground across the room and watch your dog solve the problem if you can. This frees up her safe space enough for her to focus on her task without having you standing over her or too close for comfort. This little task can be repeated in many different ways, simply by folding the towel differently and giving your dog a new slightly harder task to find the food, at a pace she can manage.

There are also tools you can use for soft sniffing, for example snuffle mats are made from felt or other material cut in strips and created to make the food hide between the strips, to make foraging and sniffing easy and rewarding. Choose your snuffle mats carefully though as many are being created based on the original but are lower quality and not as much fun. Some have stiff felt and others get worn out very easily. The other option is to get lots of felt or other materials and a good holey doormat and make your own.

Another option for soft sniffing is the Pickpocket. Holly was kindly gifted a pickpocket that she loves after she was attacked. The gift came from the creator of the idea and the product, Kate. Pickpockets are fantastic and as your dog gets braver you can fill the pockets and cover the whole thing with a towel, to enhance the task. I'll pop the website in the resources at the back of the book.

When your dog can find food in soft things, such as towels, mats, and pickpockets you can move onto problem solving with soft things. For example, I sometimes put food in old odd socks (and don't we all have plenty of those) and the dogs will work on them for ages trying to get the food out.

It's interesting to see how dogs approach things differently and how different they are in the encouragement they need.

Some need a bit of vocal encouragement or they give up. Others find it distracting or ignore the background noise altogether. Holly couldn't care less about anything when she's working around a set of problems prepared in her favourite place. She just gets on with it.

 Here she is on a winter's morning in front of her halogen heater, in her dressing gown with a very special sock. If you look really carefully, she has a steely glint in her eye over the sock. In no uncertain terms no one is having that precious soft treasure until she has gobbled up the precious food within.

There are a number of different things you can do with socks. One of my favourites for confidence building and moving from soft to potentially hard materials for problem solving is to pop some food in an old cardboard gravy tub then, instead of putting the lid back on, hook a sock over the end. If that's a little tough to begin with, try putting the sock in on top of the food then give it to your dog. Because she can focus on the soft material it's a good transition from soft to hard materials when solving problems.

Confidence

Confidence or lack of it is not only a human personality trait but, in many ways, defines our dogs, too. Interestingly, lack of confidence is not unique to dogs with sad backgrounds whilst huge confidence covers the dogs who have been nurtured all their lives. It's more complex than that and not only depends on the dog's individuality but also what they are attempting to do at the time. Certainly, dogs who have suffered may lack confidence in many situations, but they may be extremely confident in others. For example, a dog that is scared of other dogs may have no confidence to interact with them but lots of confidence telling them to go away. Or, like in Holly's case, she arrived with no confidence around people but lots of confidence around other dogs in the home.

She will happily stand and stare them out of a comfy spot she wants. She even learned during her very itchy times that if she scratched and made an odd whirring noise, they would move anyway. Holly also snores considerably, bless her, due to her funny squat nose so other dogs generally move away from her to sleep. I do wonder whether she disturbs their sleep or if they move for some other reason.

The beauty of confidence in any situation at all is that it can be raised by facilitating success and in many ways, this is why problem-solving works so well. Regular success leads to the expectation of success which in turn leads to a sunny and optimistic expectation. Whilst the expectation may be learned in one area of the dog's life, it will spread, particularly if we encourage successful choices and quietly ensure that our dogs actually succeed when they make them.

If your own dog is extremely low in confidence when problem solving with the simplest tasks, it's an excellent idea to make them simpler still. Get creative, test out vocal encouragement, and if it works, do it more. If you have to drop food on top of a towel to begin with that's fine, she will soon get the idea.

Another thing to ask yourself, if your dog seems to be struggling, is whether you are adding any pressure at all to the activity. If a dog is truly low in self-belief, they can find pressure anywhere and simply give in. We will talk more about this in the next chapter but remember this (whilst forgiving my repetition because it' an important point):

The trick to gaining the confidence of a scared dog is not to look at them, but to look in the same direction as them.

The use of food will help. Most dogs are motivated by food but there is a clause to this, it has to be the right kind of food. If it's a bland food or a poor-quality kibble, your dog might not see the point in trying at all. Remember that all this is new to her so the most motivating food in the beginning will create a wonderfully positive association. The dog that is motivated by something really special, manages to complete a problem to get to it and then gets rewarded not only with food but with her own success will naturally become more confident to try new things.

Food is such a good motivator because it fulfils a primary need, the need to eat. In foraging it also fills another of the dog's needs, to carry out natural behaviour. It also triggers dopamine which is a neurotransmitter associated with memory and motivation.

You may have heard the term dopamine in positive dog behaviour circles. It's literally rocket fuel for learning and is triggered by nice things. Dopamine passes through the brain via the neurons and changes the way a dog feels. It's one of a few neurotransmitters with an extremely important job for your dog's wellbeing. At the moment your dog solves a task and the little blob of cooked liver (for example) appears ready to be eaten she will get a dopamine blast. That blast is so powerful that she will remember exactly what she did to uncover that blob of smelly food and feel great about it too. Next time she's in the same situation she is highly likely to repeat what she did before and, after doing that a few times, she will be ready for a slightly more difficult task, growing in confidence and her self-belief will be starting to soar.

Some dogs love toys so much that we can trigger the same dopamine blast with a toy. This might not work for puppy farmed dogs, though, because they may never have even seen a toy.

Holly occasionally grabs one (if we shake it towards her) and throws it in the air but this is something she's learned from the other dogs, and not really her interaction of choice, whereas she would probably hike The Inca Trail in her dressing gown for a bit of liver cake in a cardboard box.

When your dog is confident to problem solve with soft tools and easy tasks you can start to raise the challenge a bit for her. This is great fun and the key is that anything goes, as long as it's within her current confidence and capability level. You don't need to spend a fortune on toys. In fact, you can create an imaginative world of life enrichment from simple things, like household recycling and general items that have outlived their use. I recently got a cheap and cheerful haul from a sale at a toy shop for less than one good quality dog toy. Be careful what you use, though, particularly if your dog might chew and swallow things. Don't take any risks with things that can pop off and fit into the dog's mouth.

Paper and plastic cups are fantastic for standing in a row with a treat in the bottom of each of them. Most dogs will either dip their heads in or knock them over to get to the food, which is a simple task.

Baby's stacking and nest cups (on the left) can have a treat between each of them, giving your dog the opportunity to pull them apart one after the other to find the food. This is particularly good because, after doing the first one, the dog will find the next few easier, which is great for confidence building. The giant Lego on the right is fantastic for laying on its side with a treat inside.

Moving from soft to hard equipment when providing your dog with problems to solve needs to be done carefully. Remember our task is to build her confidence gradually with lots of small successes.

Many of the supermarkets and household shops sell light (ball pool) balls from spring to early autumn. They are great for foraging in and light enough not to make lots of sudden noises which could spook a sensitive dog. Just popping them into an empty box with some tasty food sprinkled through is great progress from a snuffle mat.

A Note on Noses

Dogs have three general face shapes. The first is long, like the hound. The second is what we would consider general, like a Labrador or German Shepherd. The third is a face shape that has been created as part of artificial selection and gives the appearance of being a flat face, like the Pug or English Bulldog. This particular face shape can cause quite serious breathing issues for the dog because the nasal passages are hindered by the flattened nose. Puppy farmed dogs are usually not genetically sound anyway and health problems are likely to occur if they choose to further breed this type of dog.

It's important to bear this in mind if you have a dog breed with a round head and flat face, because they can tire easily and particularly if they are scenting for food. Breathing literally fuels the cells with oxygen all around the body and laboured breathing can cause all sorts of health problems. Although not all dogs of this type struggle, some can, so it's vital not to let them overheat and to take both exercise and enrichment (through problem solving) with them at a gentle and watchful pace.

Increasing Difficulty

When you move onto more difficult tasks for your dog to solve, you may want to consider some of the interactive toys available. Everything from food dispensing balls to electronic treat release timers are available for dogs, because as guardians we have embraced the idea of life enrichment for dogs – which is wonderful.

We can also start adding other elements into the tasks we create, for example a lot of toys in a box may rattle when the dog forages in them, which is good for confidence building because it adds another sensory element to the experience of achievement. There are so many things we can do with boxes, food wrappings, cardboard tubes, old worn out clothes, and many other safe yet otherwise useless items that we can create a whole world of canine enrichment without spending a penny.

You may want to set out a number of different tasks so your dog can work through them, when she's ready. It's vital to remember that everything must be manageable for her, but not too manageable, or it won't build her confidence. The beauty of this type of life enrichment is that there is no direct request, no expectation, and we don't have to wait until our scared dog is less scared of interacting with us, before we help her to become more confident in general.

Holly is not the only dog in our home who has grown through problem solving; all four of them now have the confidence associated with self-driven success. The result of creating suitable problems for our dogs to solve is amazing and simply can't be overstated

Chapter Eight:
Emotion and Learning

"Everything I know I learned from dogs."
–Nora Roberts

The term dog training has a lot of different approaches linked with it, in these times of big education and change. We sadly still see brutal methods and tools used in the name of dog training, we also see gentle science and understanding. When a new dog guardian looks for a dog trainer, they (and their dog) are at the mercy of an unregulated industry. Lack of regulation does not necessarily mean low quality – in all cases – but it does mean low quality in some.

As we have already explored, the dominance theory associated with domestic dogs is entirely wrong. Yet like an urban legend it lingers, woven through our lives with our dogs, on misguided television programs and perpetuated by people who call themselves dog trainers but should know much better. Thankfully things are changing, organisation are pushing for regulation and a new generation of empathy and education-driven dog professionals are emerging. It's the methods and ethics used by the new generation that I use, and that I will be teaching you here.

You might be surprised but the way that dogs learn is spookily similar to the way that we learn. Gone are the days where we believed that dogs were some raging, power hungry wolf in a woolly blanket trying to take over the world with a mind and motivation of total enigma. Here are the times where we can study the psychology associated with the gentleness of the human mind and see direct correlations with the mind of the dog.

I have studied psychology for both dogs and people, along with behaviour modification techniques used by experts in both and there is no enigma. We share so many similarities with the domestic dog that when we accept that, we can empathise with them perfectly. The idea that we need someone else to interpret our dog's pack structure behaviour, and that person tells us we must be a firm leader, is yesterday's fiction. Now we know that dogs have brain areas that light up with glee when a person they love comes along. We know that the same methods of gentle behaviour modification, adapted to incorporate lack of verbal communication, will help dogs, just as it does people.

When I look at Holly now, with an awareness of what she spent the first half of her life doing, I am amazed at the natural resilience she shows. Whilst reproduction is nature's aim, there is no doubt that mothers and their young bond. Holly has lost so many babies that she nurtured and cared for and lost them in such a brutal way. I imagine that this life was her normal. When a human mom loses a child, we never really get over it. The emotional toil, the missed years and crippling sadness pop back across the years like any other grief, even if we never met the child that was already assumed part of our future.

I'm not saying that Holly's experience is like our own, because we are obviously a different species, with different viewpoints on just about everything there is to have. I'm just pointing out that whilst we are so very different, it would be arrogant to assume that humans are the only ones that experience a strong and emotional bond with our babies. Ignoring that bond is part of what we do to other animals, and it's how we treat puppy farmed dogs.

A somewhat harrowing experience I have with the strength of canine motherhood was a long time ago but still haunts me now. During my younger years I served in the British Army as a search dog trainer and one of my postings was Kosovo in 1999. I lived in an abandoned police station with a team of British military police and my search dog, Jude. The country at that point was chaos and the Serbian army had been forced to retreat as NATO intervened.

Dogs in the Balkans were street dogs and bred like street dogs. Over the road from the police station in a burned-out car and garage, a mother dog had given birth to her litter of puppies. I started feeding and providing a bed for her new little family and checking them regularly. One day, someone approached me with advice to check the puppies. I discovered that the entire litter had been killed and set alight. That night the mother stood over her lost puppies and cried. I have never heard anything like that vocalised raw pain before or since. Her anguish punctured the night air and there was absolutely no doubt that her heart was broken. So was mine.

To assume that other animals can't experience the strong bond we feel with our children is arrogant and I would go so far as to say unkind. And if the Kosovan dog's response was indicative of emotional pain, which I believe it was. I expect puppy farm mothers suffer through enforced, repeated motherhood, too.

Canine Emotion

Emotions are created as part of the synapse. When a neural pathway is being formed and the synapse in the brain fires, it creates the chemical of emotion. The specific emotion depends on the dog and the trigger. However, when it's been created the emotion does not stay in the brain but is sent by the brain all around the body. A strong emotion that's triggered time and again will spend so much time in the body that it literally becomes part of the biological process. With this in mind, for a dog that's scared often – fear can become part of her biology. So, the dog is living in the biology of her past where times were indeed scary. This is part of the reason she can't simply shake off her experiences now she's in a new and safe home.

The reason for emotions are a mystery even within the study of people. In hard science some people believe that emotions are no more than a strong survival mechanism. We do know that they are strong, sometimes crippling, and that treatment for mental health and illness is built around the emotional lives of people.

As part of the enigma of emotional experiences, even us humans don't really know whether we experience emotions in the same way as each other. For example, if I feel happy and try to explain how that feels to you, I simply won't be able to find the words to do it without using emotional language such as elated, excited, or pleased.

We have to be a little careful about canine emotion and how much we assume about what our dogs experience, but we can certainly assume that other animals have emotions – because we are also animals after all. We are careful not to assume too much simply because we are not dogs and dogs are not people. There's a practice called anthropomorphism that means attaching human emotions onto non-humans. Some consider it a swear word and a practice to be avoided at all costs, others consider it a useful language of understanding. I tend to agree with the latter. When used sensibly we can learn a lot about how a dog feels. We can also better practice empathy when we can relate to them on a more than theoretical level.

We can pretty much safely assume that dogs have a range of basic emotions including joy, fear, anger, pain, and grief. Anyone who has lived with a dog and learned their individual nuances will agree that they are emotional animals with individuality and personality. There have been a few studies recently that give us some idea of emotions that dogs experience, including the work of Gregory Berns, and his brain scanning for dogs who are awake and aware. The findings of which showed emotional areas of the brain associated with the voice and presence of their human friend along with much more.

Complex emotions and dogs have the risk of not only being misrepresented but misinterpreted. For example, a common point of discussion is the dog who is assumed to look guilty, therefore feel guilty. We see this particular assumption all over social media, with dog shaming and similar sites. In most cases the dogs in these pictures and videos are not showing guilt but are showing anxiety and sometimes outright fear. So, whilst we don't know whether dogs experience guilt – which is in fact a mostly pointless emotion that puts us humans through lots of unnecessary pain – we can be certain that their reactions on these videos are based on an anxious response to the person photographing or filming them, not the behaviour they are supposed to be regretting.

Holly still experiences fear and anxiety. She is much happier inside her home than out in the world so her emotional responses at home are often excitement, happiness, desire to play, and sometimes unease. Out in the world she can experience anxiety, fear, and panic if loose dogs run up to us and try to sniff her whilst I'm holding her out of reach. She will experience short bursts of happiness and excitement on walks, usually when we are so far away from anything and anyone else that we seem to be the only ones on the planet.

When a worried rescue dog arrives in a new home, they often spend a lot of time being scared. Fear is their default emotional state. A healthy dog, though, that has never known fear will usually have a default state of no real strong emotion. They may be relaxed or neutral, only becoming animated or worried if something in the environment changes the way they feel. This is a vitally important point to remember, because when a scared dog comes into a home, they have to rebalance back to being a relaxed and neutral dog in their own time, then we can begin to see the happiness shine through, too. An example of this was when Holly first arrived and was tense throughout the day. Then at bedtime, as the lights went out and everyone stopped moving around, Holly would truly relax. The next day from her state of relaxation my little dog would wake up in a comfortable bed and show happiness, dancing into the day – the happiness was possible because first she had relaxed. Which is another reason why relaxation is the name of the game, at least for the first few weeks.

Emotions and learning are directly related. A dog that is scared or stressed will be hindered in her learning by the presence of cortisol – which is the hormone related directly to stress. A dog who is happy will be helped to learn by the presence of dopamine.

How Dogs Learn

Dogs are like people and learn at their own individual pace, and in a way that suits them best as the unique animal they are. Whilst individuality dictates some of their approach to learning new things, there is a general learning theory that we can consider when trying to best understand our dogs.

There's a lot of scientific jargon on learning theory, which I'm not going to go into in this book. I am however going to explain it in less scientific terms because it's important to know and will hugely raise your understanding on how dogs learn.

Gathering Clues

All dogs learn from their natural environment and things that occur within it. They are experts at stringing a number of clues together after only seeing them a handful of times. Clues that they then fast forward to an expected end result. In fact, dogs would be excellent detectives because by the time we are three or four steps away from a final act in a regularly used routine, they often already know what we are going to do. An example of this is Holly who we already know loves to forage and watches carefully for any clues that a session of food finding is on the horizon in the near future.

Once a day I go through a similar routine. Find the day's allocated forage food, stand at the counter in the kitchen and cut it up into tiny bits, shut myself in the dog's playroom for around twenty minutes and then open the door to their challenges. Holly appears the moment I fetch food out of the fridge and hangs around scraping doors until the playroom is open for business. She obviously knows where the fridge opening is going to lead and certainly comes running when the playroom door opens, no matter where she is in the house.

Every little clue to an end result will be learned by your dog. This is applicable whether your dog is learning fear or fun. The more motivated she is, the quicker she will learn but she will learn your routines, nonetheless. Whilst this lesson for

Holly is fun, the process of learning by clues applies to all learning in all situations.

Our little Yorkie cross Pomeranian is particularly astute and learns much from clues, to the point that sometimes even we need to stop and ask ourselves what she has realised. Posy (as we call our delicious little lady) watches our feet for shoes, because she knows when feet are covered that someone may be going somewhere. We actually have to carry out a shoe-removing ritual after walks before Posy will actually relax. Other examples of learning through clues include a dog refusing to go into a particular house because a smoke alarm went off in there just once, the clue being the house's front door. Or the dog that knows the sound of a laptop clicking closed means that it's time for their venture into the exciting world.

As you get to know your own dog and they begin to truly relax in your company; watch out for learning by clues. Imagine every clue she learns to pick up on is a link in a chain that your dog is building in her mind, to work out what you are going to do next. Dogs are amazing people watchers, better than we could ever imagine, particularly if they are motivated by a strong emotion of their own. Dogs even watch and respond to the smallest signals on a human face, because these signals show changes happening in our mental state, that we haven't even realised are happening yet.

Choices and Consequences

Part of the reason that dogs learn by clues is because they learn by consequences. Either consequences by things pairing up in the environment they are in, or by things that happen which they consider the consequence of their own choices. For example, a dog who is attacked by another dog can easily learn that another dog in the environment means that something terrifying is due. Or if a dog's metal collar tag hits a metal bowl and scares them, whilst they eat, that dog may learn that their choice to eat made something scary happen.

When our dogs are problem-solving they learn that the choices they make may lead to the food becoming available, or they may not. This is empowering because that choice is theirs to make, they can also learn through trial and error when problem solving. So, if their first choice doesn't work, they can try a second one, and so on. For example, if I were to give Holly a tub with a sock on, that contains her much coveted food, she will initially try a few different things to get the food out. She might throw the whole thing in the air, shake it, poke it with a paw, or walk away and go back to it. Each thing she tries originated as a choice in her mind that she puts into action.

At some point Holly will put her front paw on the tub and pull the sock off with her mouth, and out pops the food. Her correct choice was rewarded and next time she might try it earlier. When choices are successful, they are repeated and become the first choice. This is as true for problem solving as it is for any other learning experience. When something becomes the first choice every time, it now has its own neural pathway, so it becomes the default choice.

This example is the basis of all your dog's learning experiences that will fall into one of the following two groups which your dog sees as either:

"Something happens that makes something else happen".

(For science minds this is termed classical conditioning as discovered by Pavlov and his dogs)

Or

"I make a choice about something and I make something happen"

(Again, for the science minds amongst us this is Operant Conditioning as taught by Skinner based on the work of Thorndyke)

The second part of learning, the one where the dog associates her choice with an event in the environment, can be further split, which is something we will discuss in more detail in the next chapter.

So far, we know that dogs learn from things that happen in the environment inclusive of things that happen to them by something in the environment. We also know that dogs link their own choices with environmental changes. Let's take a look at how they learn to get used to something, to be sensitive about something, and how they learn preferences of environment.

When your dog gets to your home, she might at first be jumpy and scared of everything. Or she might do what Holly did and feel everything inside but not show us anything beyond learned helplessness. Initially she might only feel secure in her own bed (like Holly did when we all went to bed at night, and she went into her crate). Then she might feel secure out of her crate and on the top floor of your house because it's quieter up there and there are no doors to the outside world. If her new home is consistently a place of safety for her, your dog will get used to it and feel eventually secure wherever she is in your home. This is because she has generalised her safe feeling to a bigger area – the size of your house.

If she feels safe in your house, your dog may then generalise that safe feeling to your garden and even your car. So, if she's in these places, she will feel safe, but if she's outside them she might not.

It would be wonderful if I could tell you that generalisation will definitely spread to all possible areas of your dog's life, to walks and café's, for example. To be perfectly honest though I wouldn't be telling you the entire truth because most puppy farm escapees will always have some special quirks and, unfortunately, because they have been so socially deprived, they are likely never to be fully happy in new social situations.

Social Competence

Social skills are predominantly learned, and social wellness is based on social skills. Emotional health and psychological wellbeing are directly affected by a dog's social competence.

The current living environment of a domestic dog dictates that she not only gets along with other dogs and people, but all manner of machinery, different animals, squealing children, cats, horses, and many more unusual events. This is why good puppy trainers place much more emphasis on socialisation than training during the first few months of a puppy's life. The brain is developing and changing so much from birth to four months that we must take that window of opportunity to create a basis of confidence and bravery in the developing social capacity of our dogs.

Lack of positive social learning is one of the main reasons that we have so many worried, anxious, reactive, and hyperactive domestic dogs in our lives. In many countries, dogs have the opportunity to learn from each other by lots of contact with older dogs, throughout their puppyhood. Street dogs teach each other how to live in the world, naturally. Yet as people get involved, we so often get it wrong. Sometimes we don't realise that we are having an adverse effect on the social skills of our dogs, we are just trying our best. Other times, and in the case of puppy farmers that keep parent dogs, they simply just don't care.

There are two ways that a dog can be affected through poor social learning, the first is not to learn anything about the world at all. The second is to learn about the world but then be isolated from it, resulting in loss of previously learned social skills. Either of these can affect a dog's wellbeing to the point where even the simplest new social experience can cause extreme stress. Either can also be relevant to the lives of our rescued scared dogs.

Our task as puppy farm rescuers is to work out what exactly our dogs can cope with and accept what they can't. We can balance that out with confidence building, kind coaching, and empowerment. We can even build excellent new neural pathways. We have to accept, though, that all dogs will have strengths and areas where they are weaker. As their guardians, it's our job to recognise what they can cope with and protect them from the things they can't – at least until they are emotionally stronger.

Getting Used to Things

There is the possibility that your dog might startle at something to begin with then over time get used to it. There's also a chance that she startles at it and then becomes scared of it in the long-term.

Whether a dog becomes relaxed around a certain occurrence or scared of it really depends on the dog, their history, the occurrence, and what else is happening at the time. It also to an extent depends on their natural resilience and how quickly they recover from exposure to the occurrence (which is usually a trigger of some sort).

A dog who is highly, naturally resilient like Holly, who has been in a secure home for a while, may cope much better than a dog who has less natural resilience with the same trigger.

For example, our sound-sensitive dog Chips has always struggled with anxiety. If he hears a sound that he can't cope with, Chips will react. Holly, however, will show some interest in his reaction but doesn't do what he does, because the unusual sound has less of an effect on her. She might hear it differently as her hearing is patchy and Chips hears everything, but she also cares about it much less than he does, because Holly in her home is now an extremely resilient little dog.

When a dog learns about something new, either through changes in the environment or changes that she believes are caused by her choices, it's like a snapshot in time. Remember the old polaroid cameras that took a picture then spat it out of the front for us to wave around whilst it develops? Try to imagine that your dog's learning experience is just like that snapshot. Everything in the environment at the time will be part of the learning experience for your dog.

If you have ever studied NLP, you will be aware that this is also the case for humans. If you don't know much about the practice, here's a superfast lesson. NLP tells us that we gather information through three main areas, sight, hearing, and touch. In the same way, our dogs will be gathering information through their direct senses but theirs includes scent, because they have an amazing nose. In fact, their sense of scent is considered their primary sense. So, your dog might smell, see, hear, and be touched all in one moment and that moment becomes her learning experience of it.

A common example is the smell, sight, and sound of the veterinarian's office that also results in being touched. Most scared dogs will class the act of being touched by a stranger as pretty stressful. So, the moment your dog is in the vet's office, with the smell, the sight, and the sound of everything she is there with, then she gets touched – that's what she has learned. This is often why dogs realise they are at the entrance to the vets and try to double back and go home. In this case if a fear develops the dog can consider to be sensitised to the vets.

When our dogs get used to an area then learn to relax within it, they have become habituated to it (they have got used to it and relaxed). This can happen quickly or take time. Our dogs generally always habituate to our homes, as it's the place they learn to relax in. If a puppy farm rescue becomes sensitised to her new home that's a really sad event and the dog will need professional help and perhaps even medication from the veterinarian.

It's a good idea to watch your dog carefully and be aware of what's happening in her environment that may be affecting her at any given time. By doing this you can begin to truly understand how she is coping with the world. Enlightened observation will also help you to help her when she needs it, recognise any onset of stress, and prevent prolonged fear. When you can see that something is worrying your dog, you have more options. You can tell the worrying thing to back off or simply turn tail and get her out of there; whip your delicate dog away, like a true hero ninja warrior!

Chapter Nine: Canine Coaching

"The gift which I am sending you is called a dog, and is in fact the most precious and valuable possession of mankind" –Theodorus Gaza

Canine coaching is a gentler term than dog training. The coach brings out the best of the dog, that's already in there, by gently teasing her natural abilities and providing empowerment through choices, learning, and success.

Rescuing a puppy farm dog often means that they are older and have never really experienced any kind of learning process, other than helplessness in many cases. You may not even be interested in teaching your dog new things for the sake of it. I generally don't teach tricks or obedience to any of my dogs. We just share the world with fun, enrichment, and necessary lessons for life. The aim with canine coaching can be to use your dog's brain to her best and happiest life. It's particularly important for dog breeds that have a lot of mental energy but can benefit everyone and most importantly coaching can help with general husbandry by making it less of a scary challenge for your dog.

It's a myth that old dogs can't learn new tricks. Dogs can learn new things at any time in their life, due to neuroplasticity. They may not learn as quickly and they may not be interested in complex lessons, but all dogs of all ages can learn suitable lessons and to do so will benefit them greatly. Neuroplasticity is the brain's capacity to create new neural pathways which naturally support new choices and habits. When we provide our dogs with learning opportunities, we are keeping their capacity for new thoughts, choices, and feelings well and truly open. We are literally keeping them young.

One positive aspect about rescuing a puppy farm parent dog is how often they revert to puppyhood after settling into their new life. It's really interesting to watch this happen and extremely rewarding. It resembles a rebirth where the puppy they were always meant to be comes bubbling to the surface. I think puppy farm dogs actually get mentally younger in their new home, over the course of a few months. During this chapter I'm going to cover how to teach dogs new things. We will explore the relevant science in an accessible way, to help you understand how to best guide your dog to learn, using kindness and understanding every step of the way.

Coaching a scared dog is a unique process and extremely rewarding. It may be slower than when we teach a bright and confident puppy, but all dogs learn in the same way and when we can get the communication right, reinforcement works as well for worriers as it does for everyone else.

Reinforcement is based on the learning process that I described earlier. Specifically, the dog's idea that something they did elicited a response from the environment. When we teach something, within a method of direct communication, we become the direct environment. For example, after a few months of being with us Holly learned to sit for a treat. There was no real reason for the sit position in her case. We were not asking anything from her, it just became easy to teach because she tried it once and the reinforcement began.

Holly likes it when we sit on the ground. It's a pleasant experience for her because she has learned that tiny treats are out onto outstretched legs, gently and quietly, which she then takes. It has all been part of her getting used to people, and if your own dog is scared of hands, I recommend you try sitting on the ground and popping food on your legs. It's something so simple but can be a great confidence builder.

As I was saying, Holly likes it very much when we sit on the ground. Not only because food usually arrives but also because deep down, she really likes one on one attention. She has that same addiction to human interaction that every dog is born with, it's just that hers is focussed only on us which is a precious privilege! Some dogs will interact with anyone who looks their way. When the food didn't arrive on my leg as she was used to, Holly backed up a bit and decided what to do next. She made a choice and sat so I dropped a bit of food in front of her. In Holly's mind she made that food happen, simply by sitting.

In her body a lot of things were happening at the same time. Her neurons fired into the beginning of a neural pathway. Dopamine was triggered by the food reward and because of the dopamine she remembered what she did for the food. She is also likely to have experienced a glimmer of self-belief.

I helped her naturally out of the chosen sit position by popping the food just out of her reach. She's a bright and keen dog so I waited, and she tried it again, and again the food arrived. Before I knew it, Holly was sitting over and over again. She's become a champion sitter without even hearing the word.

When we have started marking choices, we can then give them a unique name of their own. For example, just as Holly sat on her own and before I marked that choice, I used the word "sit" and she soon learned that the word was associated with her choice and ultimately her reward. When we add a word to a specific choice, we can put that choice on cue, with careful practice. We do this by introducing the cue as the behaviour happens – until the dog knows the association – we then bring the cue forward so when she hears it, she associated it with the choice, eventually making that choice on cue.

The process that Holly learned to sit through is called positive reinforcement. She tried something and the environment (I, in this case) rewarded it by adding something that she liked into our shared experience, but for her alone. Positive reinforcement is empowering for all dogs, because within it there is not a jot of force. For scared dogs who have learned helplessness it's absolutely wonderful.

The very basis of this method is "something good happens". When that good thing happens, learning occurs. There are a number of tools we can use within positive reinforcement. They are pretty simple responses and techniques that make communication easier and break down learning into even gentler chunks.

Alongside providing the food reward, we can mark a dog's choice with a specific sound or word. A traditional marker is a clicker, but for scared dogs, clicking may be too much. Yet a word delivered in a low tone will do a fantastic job without making your dog jump – "good" is an excellent word. A marker is a bridge between the choice your dog makes and the food she receives. It is used to make the connection a little clearer to the dog, and to reinforce a certain choice when you may not be able to provide food at the exact moment they make the choice.

For the marker to be truly effective it needs to be connected to the delivery of food in your dog's mind. This is easy. You can simply say the word and drop the food a few times, over a few sessions over a few days. Then soon enough your dog will hear that word and expect the food. Remember when you say the marker word, after your dog has learned the connection with food, she will expect food every time she hears it. Choose your word carefully.

Why We Use Food

You may have heard people say that food is bribery, that dogs should not be taught with food but learn out of respect or other similar things. Unfortunately, they are out there and often the same people use punishment or force to threaten dogs into complying, where the enlightened ones amongst us just use the power of food. We use food because it's a fantastic motivator. It triggers good feelings, it's rewarding, and food is downright pleasant for the dog.

When we use food to elicit and reward a behaviour we are working with the wonder of the dog's brain. It's basic positive reinforcement and makes learning easy, fun, and fast. Motivation is the basis of all behaviour change. Every single choice has an intention attached to it and the stronger the intention is the quicker that choice will be learned. For example, Holly had an intention to get me to drop a treat in front of her. She learned that choosing to sit achieved her aim and got her that much coveted food. She hadn't woken up that morning with an intention to learn to sit; she didn't even intend to learn to sit at the point she started sitting. Yet when she saw that I had some food, her intention was to elicit that food, the choice to sit was a side effect.

Let's consider a different dog in a different situation, an altogether less pleasant one. Imagine Ron the dog trainer who is trying to teach a dog to sit. Ron hasn't learned the power of a positive intention, so he starts his session by telling the dog to sit. Understandably the dog hasn't a clue what "sit" means so Ron pushes her down into a sit position. Now the dog is likely a bit stressed because no-one wants to be pushed around, yet she still doesn't know what is expected of her. Ron, because he's shown the dog by pushing her a few times, believes that she knows what "sit" means so starts to get frustrated at the dog's "defiance". Take a moment now and ask yourself what you think the dog's one and only intention will be in this situation.

If you said to get away from Ron the dog trainer, I heartily agree. Eventually if he keeps acting like a brute towards her Ron will trigger the dog's fight or flight system. He might get bitten or he might break the dog's spirit and force her into learned helplessness. He certainly hasn't motivated her or taught her anything other than the fact that he's a bully.

Sadly, the dog training world still has too many Rons in it, yet the number of people who know and do better is growing every day. And you are part of the positive movement now, too – welcome!

Capturing Choices

When a marker is established, we can use it to capture natural choices that our dogs make. This is perfect for scared dogs because we don't actually ever ask them to do anything at all. We simply wait for them to make a useful choice and mark then reward it. As we know, a choice rewarded is likely to be repeated and repetition leads to the neural pathway, finally becoming the default choice. And it's all doused in beautiful dopamine - how amazing is that?

You can use your marker for problem solving, then reinforce the act of peeing outdoors or even when your dog moves closer to you and stays relaxed. In fact, marking relaxation is a wonderful way to increase it because whilst it's not a choice as such and the dog is unlikely to think, "I'll relax again for another reward," she will naturally go from relaxed to rewarded, which is a fantastic process to build from. When you have practiced the skill of capturing choices and relaxation, you can start to stretch your dog's comfort zone a little bit in the same way.

After Holly had got to the point where she sat and waited for the food, I began to mark the sit with a word and added in something new. I started moving my hands around her before delivering the marker and food. This was done extremely carefully because hands are very scary things and moving hands take scared dogs well out of their comfort zone. The process of sit – mark – treat became sit – mark – move other hand – then treat. And it worked, Holly would stay sitting whilst I moved my scary hand in front of her tiny face.

The reason it worked so well is because I didn't expect too much too soon. I moved my hand just enough, a tiny bit more each day. Within her comfort zone and ability to cope but still just enough to grow her confidence each time. That's what you're aiming for with everything you teach to your own dog. Just enough to stretch their capability to cope but not enough to trigger a response of fear or confusion. You may have some false starts, because the art of "just enough" is a learned skill, but dogs are forgiving, and each practice session will build your bond.

Touch

Touch is a necessary part of caring for our dogs. We have to touch them for health, cleanliness, and husbandry. Often, we have to touch them when they are scared, too, although with practice we can make it easier for them.

When your marker is established, and your dog is used to moving hands you can begin to touch her then mark her relaxation. Whilst we can't avoid necessary touches before this learning experience, we can make a difference in how our dog is feeling in the long-term. When we teach relaxation whilst being touched, it will spread into all areas of necessary touch in the life of the dog.

The key is to do it at the dog's pace then to practice regularly. There are four stages of learning something new and before your friend is completely happy with being touched, she must go through these stages. They go like this:

1. The first experience of the lesson, gaining the information.
2. Becoming good at the lesson.
3. Practicing the lesson in many ways.
4. Making the lesson part of their learned behaviour as default.

In the case of teaching your dog that touch is both normal and relaxing you can start at a slow pace and use your marker along the way. Your dog will soon realise - in the same way as Holly did with my hand movements - that a marker and reward is on the way. You might need to use the back of your hands initially, as they are not the grabby bits and your scared friend might be able to accept them more readily.

The trick with this is to ensure you deliver your marker very quickly in the beginning. Any withholding of that sound and the fear reaction could creep in. If it helps, imagine your marker as a baseball bat and the fear your dog might experience as the ball, flying towards her. Your marker will hit that ball (fear) into the next field if it's delivered repeatedly at the right time. As you send the fear flying, it will be naturally delivered less often, and you can wait a couple of seconds longer before delivering the marker and reward.

As your dog starts to learn that touch is actually a prelude to something amazing, she will become gradually good at accepting it. How quickly this happens depends on her individuality.

Next you can generalise the touch by touching her on different parts of her body. For example, start to touch her ears, feet, and mouth but keep using your marker and batting away that fear. Always moving at your dog's relaxed pace and keeping her within her comfortable zone.

Finally, just practice this until your dog is happy to be touched. It might take a very long time but it's well worth the effort and is exceptional for bonding. And when your dog is happy to be touched you can use that for the most effective touch of all – TTouch.

Health Checking

Health checking is important for all dogs but it's vital for the escapees of puppy farms. Their early days contained little to no healthcare and it is usually adulthood to senior years when this starts to show in the physical body. To carry out an effective health check – whilst also keeping your dog relaxed - might take regular practice over a lot of sessions. But keep gently progressing and marking your dog's progress and you simply can't fail. It's a good idea to start at the eyes and work to your dog's tail, gently and methodically.

Eye health includes checking for discharge and cloudiness. Cataracts may develop as the dog gets older and she might not have great sight to begin with, if she spent her first few years in a dark puppy farm. Cataracts look pretty distinctive. They appear cloudy and milky but often they develop on older dogs as they enter their senior years. Long-haired dogs might get lumps of eye discharge stuck in the hair under their eyes. Warm water on cotton wool balls will soften this

 discharge and allow you to wipe it away.

Check ears for small discharge and watch your dog for any excessive scratching which can indicate mites or infection. When Holly arrived with us, she had no hair on her ears

at all. They were like little triangles of bald skin. Her fosterer told me that it was usual for farmed dogs and part of a response to fungus. The hair does grow back, though, and when Holly's ear hair started growing, I thought it was never going to stop. The above picture was taken when Holly was still with her fosterer. Shiny ears and eyes that still saw the puppy farm. The second one is half asleep with us – look at all that amazing hair!

Gently lift your dog's lips and check the teeth on both sides. Then when she's ready to accept it, open her mouth to look inside. Small dogs are more prone to tartar build up, wobbly teeth, and tooth infections. A build-up of bacteria in the mouth can spread and cause infections elsewhere in the body. Some dogs may require their teeth to be professionally cleaned under a general anaesthetic. Sometimes rescues do this before rehoming puppy farm dogs.

Run your hands over her checking for any lumps. In female dogs remember to feel along the mammary glands to check for any abnormal swellings, which can be a sign of mammary cancer. Holly had a little mammary lump taken off her stomach about a year after joining us.

Also, look for any scabs, irritations, or areas of hair loss. Hotspots are areas of the skin that become especially sore and dogs often chew or excessively lick them. Hotspots may be the sign of allergy to food and a natural immune response of a problem that hasn't really been dealt with. The first step with a hotspot is the veterinarian. If you can find a holistic vet that's great as they tend to explore the underlying reason for the immune response, whereas others may focus on treating the symptoms which could stop the scratching but won't deal with the underlying issue.

Check your dog's nails, because if they get too long it can affect your dog's posture. Clipping nails regularly and brushing teeth daily can become part of your dog's normal care routine, particularly if you coach carefully so she's relaxed whilst you do it. Again, simply break down the end process into smaller steps and mark all relaxed behaviour whilst simultaneously batting that fear beast away!

Replacing Unwanted Choices

Whilst choices are empowering and great for our worried dogs, they may sometimes not make the best ones for us and them. For example, eating things that are not great for their health, wellbeing, or breath.

Coprophagia is common in dogs that have escaped the puppy farm. Coprophagia is a polite way to describe eating poo. Holly likes a tasty poo and without getting to it quickly whilst watching her carefully she will indeed gobble up a whole one. I have an amusing memory of my husband fiddling with poo bags and Holly racing up and inhaling the prize before he could whip it away, his face was a picture – and a bit green. Eating poo can occur for many reasons. Just like any choice it can occur as a habit, for fun, out of desperation, or because of something happening within the dog's body, such as (mental or physical) illness or nutrient deficiency. It's important to look at why it happens, for any unusual act or choice.

Choices are at their most empowering when they are also good for the dog. The good news is that we can change almost any choice by facilitating a better one that's even more rewarding for the dog. In its most basic form, if I offer something to Holly that she prefers to those habitually coveted tasty poos she likes so much, she will choose my offering instead.

There are three maintaining factors for any choice that your dog makes. The first is what happens directly before the choice, the second is the choice itself, and the third is the what happens directly after she makes it. Our job is not only to work out why that is the default choice but also to tweak the environment so the dog can make a healthier one.

A dog that wees in the house for example might be making the choice to go on the deep pile rug on a regular basis. Whilst her chosen corner of the rug is now less pile than it is enzymatic cleaner, we can't seem to stop that little patch of pee reoccurring. It's a good idea to look at the bigger picture of the choice she is making, including the three factors that directly affect her choices. The details of before, during, and after her squirt.

When we watch carefully, we catch details that we may have missed before. Most dogs give us a clue before they pee in the house, it's just that their clues may be small and unless we have a sharp eye, we can miss them. They might get up and move, glance towards us or sniff the ground. This is the prelude to their act. When we recognise the prelude, we can foretell the act itself.

It's that moment of awareness where we must facilitate a better choice and provide that choice with a much more attractive consequence. So, we might cheerily lead our friend outside - or if necessary and the dog is not too stressed by touch we may have to taxi them a few times - then when they choose to pee in the garden instead, we provide a consequence that's extremely rewarding. This is just one example where we can change the choices to more helpful ones. It works with everything. Eventually when your dog learns a new choice, she will forget about the other one, therefore stop making it altogether.

The Damage of Punishment

I had a message recently from a lady who had booked a (seemingly well-respected) dog trainer to see her reactive dog. After the appointment was booked, the trainer asked the lady to measure her dog's neck for a chain, because he might use one "depending how bad the behaviour is". The trainer was planning to punish the dog, and even more chilling (if that's possible) he was planning to punish a dog he hadn't even met. Punishment is old school dog training. To use punishment betrays a lack of education and empathy. It certainly works when delivered correctly but even then, it's confusing and cruel.

In the words of one particular renowned dog behaviourist:

"To use shock as an effective dog training method you will need:

> *A thorough understanding of canine behaviour.*
> *A thorough understanding of learning theory.*
> *Impeccable timing.*

And if you have those three things, you don't need a shock collar."

Dr Ian Dunbar

Whilst Dr Dunbar is talking specifically of electric shock as punishment, the statement above applies to all types of punishment – because punishment itself is literally based on some kind of shock, pain, or fear. There are many problems with using punishment. The first is that it relies on the dog practicing the act that we are trying to eradicate. As we already know, anything that is repeated creates a specific neural pathway. Practice makes habits.

Another issue with punishment is that it can cause suppression through fear.

For example, if I were to punish a dog every time she pulled on a lead, by checking her, I wouldn't be showing her what I would like her to do instead, I would just be hurting and scaring her. Eventually the dog may stop pulling but more because she is depressed than because she has learned that's what I would prefer she does.

Suppression is not only unfair, but it can be dangerous. For example, if you were in a friendship with someone and they told you to be quiet every time you attempted to speak about your needs, you may stop trying. It doesn't mean that your needs are no longer present. In fact, because they have pushed them deep inside you, they might be all you think about. When our needs are not met, even our biology becomes obsessed with them, we can think of nothing else. Eventually we may get physically ill based on all the inner turmoil, or we might reach the end of our tether and bop that particular friend on the nose.

We have the power to walk away from people who make us suppress our feelings, yet dogs can't walk away. They will either get ill and depressed, highly anxious, or do their only other choice – start to threaten us that enough is enough. Depending on the dog's personality and experience of life, threatening might or might not happen. Holly would probably never have bitten when she arrived with us, yet as she's grown into her choices, she's happier to poke us with her nose as a protest, which is brilliant, because she's starting to be empowered and realises she has at least some say in what happens to her.

Just as punishment has been identified as being bad for children, and most people will agree that sparing the rod/spoiling the child is a description of old-fashioned brutality, hopefully we will someday soon see the same enlightenment in the treatment of dogs.

Chapter Ten:
Anxiety Disorders

"Life is a series of dogs."
–George Carlin

During the final chapter we are going to look at anxiety and related disorders that dogs may suffer with, how they manifest, and how we can help them.

Anxiety is broadly defined as apprehension of potential future negative events or danger. It can be accompanied by hypervigilance and general tension. There are two categories of anxiety, situational and internally generated. This means that a dog may become anxious because something outside them, in their environment is happening. Or they could suffer with internally generated anxiety, for example Generalised Anxiety Disorder, which needs no external trigger as it begins inside the dog.

Important point: Not all puppy farm dogs, or fearful dogs in general, will have internally generated anxiety. Holly doesn't, and after nearly three years with us, when she does experience anxiety it is caused by specific external triggers. I do live with a dog who suffers with anxiety, though, and you may, too. It really depends on your dog's individual personality.

If your dog hasn't been with you for very long, you might find that she seems quite anxious now, but the longer she is there – and the more time she gets used to things in her new environment – you may learn that she isn't actually an anxious dog at all. She has just needed the time to unpack. That's not to say she will get over all external anxiety triggers, just that she doesn't self-general perpetual anxiety.

Signs of anxiety can include vigilance, scanning, tension, and responses that seem overt. Muscle tension may be common, and even when relaxed, the dog with established anxiety can become tense very quickly. Anything in the dog's environment can trigger external-based anxiety. Common types may include being left alone, sound phobias, or even simpler things such as things the dog has learned to be scared of, including other dogs. When we can recognise the trigger in the environment, we have something to work with, through general desensitisation and counter-conditioning. If there doesn't seem to be a specific trigger for anxiety, we then must consider internally created problems, for example PTSD or GAD.

Generalised Anxiety Disorder

Dogs with long-term generalised anxiety will stress weight off themselves. They may never seem to relax, always waiting for the next thing to worry about. Hypervigilance may occur in this dog, even when nothing has changed or there are no potential triggers near her. Our job is to observe so thoroughly that we can find even the smallest potential trigger and if we can't then we must consider that the dog may be creating her anxious state from the inside.

Signs of GAD include the inability to focus, easily distracted, highly reactive behaviour characterised by barking, whining, and lunging. The dog who is suffering with GAD will not be able to habituate to environment triggers; she may not even be able to habituate to home environments where there are not triggers, without being hypervigilant, sometimes for many years. Another symptom of GAD is loose bowel movements regularly, based on inflammatory bowel issues, which can be a side effect of heightened reactivity. GAD is also often linked with noise phobias, sound sensitivity, and high reactivity to sound.

Without understanding, the dog suffering with internally generated anxiety can seem to behave in a way that is hyperactive, and generally noisy, when really they are struggling on the inside and the things we see outside are just the symptoms.

How Can We Help Them?

Helping the dog suffering with long-term generalised anxiety is not easy. They can seem distracted for behaviour modification and coaching, they may not be able to hold focus and are always on the lookout (listen-out) for something to bark at. The dog may have been coping (not so) quietly with GAD all their life. It could have just been part of her life before but now she's in a place where someone might recognise it for what it actually is.

The first step is recognition, then it's a good idea to go to an excellent vet and discuss formal diagnosis and whether medication will help the dog to cope. There are a number of medication types which are used for canine mental health; often they are also used with people. Medication may be a good first step, yet it should always be used alongside changes to the environment and restriction of potential triggers. As with all medication for mental health issues, it should be used alongside a holistic plan, always discussed in detail with your veterinarian and only prescribed by a vet. Don't be tempted to dismiss medication based on any preconceptions; used at the beginning of a bigger plan it can work really well for dogs that need relief from GAD and other anxiety disorders.

As with all imbalances and conditions whether mental or physical, we must look at the basic holistic health and balance of the dog. A good diet with careful supplementation for holistic health is important.

We then have to be sure that all the dog's needs are met properly and in a way suitable to her. We can look to the Five Freedoms for this as a checklist.

The Five Freedoms of Wellness

The five freedoms were initially created to offer farmed animals a level of protection from bad practices. To ensure that their basic needs were met. Since their creation, the five freedoms have been adopted by many organisations, for general animal welfare, and when used properly they can provide us with a general guidance for the welfare of even the most complicated dog.

The five freedoms include:

1. Freedom from hunger and thirst. This can be extended beyond the basic provision of food and water by choosing a bespoke diet for the dog. In addition, we can use nutraceuticals for supplementation, to ensure extra support for wellness where the dog needs it.

2. Freedom from discomfort by providing a comfortable and safe resting area. In the case of a dog suffering

with anxiety that might mean turning on classical music to drown out sounds in the environment. The idea is to make them feel safe, even though we already know they are.

3. Freedom from pain, injury, and disease which we can do by being educated and aware of the signs of ill health – both mental and physical – then taking our dogs to the vets if they appear unwell. We can also do much more, by managing the wellbeing and everyday balance of our dogs to prevent disease beginning and progressing wherever possible.

4. Freedom to express normal behaviour which is covered perfectly by social care, enrichment, foraging, and general games which allow the dog to fulfil her natural needs to capacity.

5. Freedom from fear and distress means that we both create a safe space and environment for the dog in this life and help them to get over fears learned in the previous ones. This is particularly relevant to puppy farm dogs and dogs that have suffered at the hands of people.

It's really worth spending some time with the five statements above and working out exactly how they may fit into your own dog's life. Holly for example has been able to get beyond her previous anxieties and depression because:

1. She doesn't need to worry about where her food is coming from. She eats a freshly cooked diet of meats and vegetables with multivitamin supplements. And can always get a drink.

2. She has a number of warm and safe sleeping areas where she can truly relax, not worry about being touched and feel safe whether she's awake or asleep. She's even habituated to banging doors on the TV now.

3. Holly is healthy and taken to the vets when she needs to be.

4. She gets lots of exciting enrichment, foraging, and games. Holly's walks are short and slow enough not to overtire her but efficient enough to have built her muscles that support her joints. Her walks keep her healthy. She isn't exposed to dogs outside her own circle because they are triggers for her, yet she has a family of her own kind in her home.

5. We try hard not to scare Holly in the way we act, which has worked, and she now asks us to play regularly. She isn't forced into situations or interaction that she doesn't instigate.

This basis of wellness when carefully delivered and managed, whilst catered to your own dog, will manage her internal and external environment to prevent stress beyond what she facilitates internally. We can then see any disorder or ill health more clearly, without mixing it up with environmental stress.

Relaxation

Relaxation is difficult when a dog suffers with anxiety-related disorders, particularly if their environment is punctuated by unavoidable triggers, such as in the case of sound sensitivity and anxiety.

There are a few things we can do that will help our dogs properly relax. First, we ensure their needs are met, especially physical and mental exercise needs. Then we can start to incorporate relaxation into their lives naturally. It won't happen all at once, but like any new behaviour, learning to relax is another learning process.

To be clear, anxiety and hyperarousal are two different behaviours and there may be different reasons for them. So, we can't assume that the dog who is very energetic naturally suffers with an anxiety disorder. Similarly, we can't assume that a dog who is not highly energetic is not suffering with anxiety. Remembering that all dogs are individuals is paramount to understanding them.

Techniques for Relieving Anxiety

When we have dealt with any environmental triggers, we can introduce some careful, steadying techniques for helping an anxious dog to cope. They can include checking in with us for gentle reassurance, taking a breath and adopting body positions that naturally trigger the mind to catch up with her relaxed stance.

It's important to remember that if she's not built a bond with you, direct attention that you may focus on her may trigger her anxiety, so always start and end the small lessons at a coping point for her. One minute of doing something positive that she can call on later is much better than five minutes where she becomes worried. If she's not comfortable with one minute, then stick with the environmental anxiety relief and wait until she is.

Dr Karen Overall teaches biofeedback as a technique for coping, for dogs that are experiencing an anxiety-based response. Biofeedback can help the dog remember where she is in the space of her body. As anxiety can leave the dog spiralling out of awareness and into panic. Something simple such as taking a breath will often ground the dog back towards calmness for that moment and prevent the anxiety spiralling out of control.

General biofeedback can be something simple, such as taking a breath. Which is easy to teach with positive reinforcement.

The act of sniffing something interesting is an excellent tool for teaching a big deep breath. When your dog takes a big sniff, she will inhale not only the scent but also a lot of air.

The scent and air will split, scent goes to the memory area of the brain whilst the oxygen races around the circulatory system giving a quick burst of wellbeing.

To teach our dog to take a deep breath, we can simply hold a tasty treat and wait for the dog to take a big sniff in, marking the moment her nostrils flare and giving her the treat. The aim is to get oxygen into the circulatory system in one big gulp – that will naturally calm her mind. Oxygen will give the brain a moment of space, preventing your dog rushing into the next moment. Taking a breath can be extended so that your dog learns to hold her breath for a moment or two before the treat is given. We can then put a big breath on cue – just as I did with Holly's sit earlier.

The way that we move around and touch an anxious dog is also extremely important. Moving slowly and deliberately, keeping your tone quiet and avoiding bangs and sudden sounds will really help a dog who is anxious, particularly if she is also sound sensitive. A radio on all day long, with classical music, may help drown out some sudden sounds, which can help.

An important part of touch is consent, which is harder than it sounds but necessary. It's difficult because we people soothe by touch, yet a dog who is touched without choosing it or giving her consent will be less able to relax than one who is allowed to decide whether she is touched or not. Remember that a dog with anxiety often never fully relaxes, so to touch them when they least expect it may send them spiralling into their default anxious state. So always ask first, and if your dog say's no thank you – by offering a glance away or lip lick as a cut-off signal – respect her request and back off. This alone will build her trust in you.

With her consent, touching and stroking an anxious dog should be deliberate and long, steady strokes with no quick movements. Don't go over her head but under her chest. Any hand moving quickly and particularly in a downward motion is likely to worry her.

If your dog is anxious yet happy for the lightest touch, I highly recommend you learn at least some TTouch moves that you can use to help her to cope when she's starting to fret or show worry. Dr. Janet Finlay offers a lot of generously free information on how to use TTouch for worried dogs, and also runs some wonderful video courses on touch for calming and confidence building.

Through her course and practice of Canine Flow, Caroline Griffith teaches the energetic aspects of living and working with dogs. An interesting lesson I learned through canine flow is how dogs tend to ground their energy through their mouth area. This is a teaching I have seen in action time and again in my own dogs. We know that dogs (and of course people) are made not only of biology but also of energy, as explored and explained by the teachings of quantum physics. Canine Flow teaches that dogs experiencing a surge of energy will most likely try to ground through their mouth area. Which in my opinion fits perfectly with dogs who are stressed and seem to endlessly bark, or little puppy farm escapees who may lick their legs and feet beyond which they could possibly ever need licking.

Please do explore the section at the end of the book for references and other resources that will help you on your own journey with your dog

Holly Today

Whilst I'm sitting here finishing the end of this first draft, Holly has decided it is playtime. She's a funny dog who wakes up around three in the afternoon and dances around my office, determined for a game. She looks up at me and wriggles her body, bright eyes twinkling and her funny little half tail dancing to its full capacity.

The look on her face shows that she completely trusts me now. The nose nudge confirms it and she occupies our lives as the smallest, sparky ray of sunshine she has become. Holly has blossomed into the dog she should have been right from the beginning, and when I think about her sad little life way back before she escaped, I hope that she has forgotten all about it.

Wales, where Holly is from, has many licenced puppy farms. Packed with hundreds of little broken dogs. So please consider this and spread the word, because by buying puppies from unclear backgrounds we directly fund these farms. Rescuing one little dog won't change the world, but for that dog it does. It changes their world in a way that nothing else ever could.

If you have a Holly of your own, you have my ultimate respect. They may not be easy on our hearts but goodness they are worth it! Every new sparkle is worth it!

Thank you for joining us.

Resources

Canine Principles (caninprinciples.com) is my own family business that covers all types of canine wellness, coaching, and behaviour in online, theoretical study. We have twenty courses available on Canine Principles, over 2000 students, and all are fully tutored by a wonderfully positive team.

My other books available on Amazon can be accessed through my writer profile or my website (https://www.sallygutteridge.com). You can also contact me directly through the website or my Facebook page (facebook.com/sallyanddogs).

The Canine Confidence Academy (canineconfidenceacademy.com) which was created and is run by Dr Janet Finlay has a lot of free resources for both the reactive dog and the emotional toil that can take on trying to help dogs who struggle in the world. Janet's work is amazing, and I highly recommend signing up to her emails, and a course, if you can.

Caroline Griffith runs Canine Flow (http://thespiritualdogtrainer.com/services/) which is practitioner training and general canine understanding on energetic levels. Caroline also runs amazing Canine Flow retreats all over the world.

An excellent book mentioned in the text is the Manual of Clinical Behavioural Medicine by Dr Karen Overall, published by Elsevier. This is an amazing book designed for practitioners of clinical animal behaviour and packed with knowledge, tips, and information. It's not really a book for general pet owners as it covers so much and is a detailed textbook. Yet is a great read and reference for professionals on any level.

You can get a Pickpocket food forager, like the one that Holly was so kindly gifted, directly from Kate at the website (pickpocketforagers.com).

The original snuffle mats are available from the website which has an amazing range of confidence building sniff toys (www.rufflesnufflemats.com).

Final Note

I hope you have enjoyed the book and that it's helped you understand your own dogs just a little more. If so, would you mind leaving a review on Amazon please, as they literally make me beam like Holly does at playtime?

If you're reading this through Kindle, would you hit the star rating above too, please? (Five would be awesome). Many thanks!

I would also love to see your own dogs so if you feel like popping along to my Facebook page (www.facebook.com/sallyanddogs) with stories and pictures, I would be eternally grateful. We can never know enough dogs in our short lives, can we?

We look forward to hearing from you!

Sally and Holly!

Printed in Great
Britain
by Amazon